I0406883

Sex

and

The Cosmos:

A Counter-Intuitive Book for Parents

and 'Randy' Young Adults.

SidL

Original Title: God Loves Sex Too...

Dedication

Young adults of today—parents of tomorrow—upon whose shoulders the heavy burden of abstinence from sex is placed, by parents who just don't get it.

The Sexually suppressed.

Parents of today—young adults of yesterday—who deny their own understanding of the burden, and consequences, of abstinence from sex demanded of you as young adults, and yet perpetuate the cycle.

The Sexual suppressors.

To you both, this book is lovingly dedicated, as a call to truce.

Table of Contents

Introduction

If you have come this far, then you fall into one of four categories:

1. You are a parent.

2. You are a young adult.

3. You are a forward thinking individual already open to ideas which at first seem strange, but strangely true.

4. You are none of the above, but sufficiently curious about the outlandish, unorthodox ideas, which this book aims to seed.

To all of you, I say thank you very much for giving the benefit of a read, or two.

Thank you for offering a mind with which the soothing, healing balm of a *new and better way* of thinking may be applied to the burdened shoulders of humankind, looking for ways to solve even its most basic problems.

Sex is a big problem right now for humankind, among many other problems of course, and it need not be so. Every part of the human body has been purposefully crafted to have its needs fulfilled without drama. The penis and vagina should not be exceptions, but they are.

As it is right now, the adults of humankind are fighting the *perpetual* good fight of managing their own sexual urges, even though it need not be a battle. They cannot understand why sex holds so much power over them, why they simply cannot resist or control themselves when it comes to sex. In not knowing the *why* of it, adults obsess over it.

As long as it is understood that no person is born a sexually active adult, then it should not be difficult to understand that the source of unwholesome preoccupation with sex is traceable to the onset of puberty or sexual desires, and how it was managed. These same adults who are themselves battling with their preoccupation with sex, go on to become parents of the next generation of humankind, and the cycle is thus guaranteed to repeat itself.

May I ask, what then are you adults teaching your children who have become young adults? Do as I say, not as I do? How is that working out?

To our young adults at the glorious stage of puberty, it is sad to say that you are only *victims* of parents who were equally victims of theirs, just as your children will become your *victims*. The trend will continue unless a new way of thinking is introduced into this rather confusing equation of the sex-urge management.

What looks to humankind as a general decadence present within itself were sex is concerned is the outworking of the one law of the universe—*the law of balance*. Furthermore, a mass misconception about the true nature of what is termed *God*, is responsible for the sexual runaway that humankind is currently experiencing.

Humankind is yet to be taught en mass that no

being loves sex more than *God himself*. I will therefore set about the task of teaching you all about the true nature of *God* and *his* very, very sexual ways and processes. We will then proceed to apply this understanding—depending on how open minded you are—so that you will start to see sex in a whole new light. Young adults will be most pleased, and feel a deep sense of relief in what I will teach.

It is my intention that this book serve the purpose of establishing a truce between the obligation of parents to protect the sexual interests of their children, and the rights of children—young adults—to experience and enjoy the wonders, beauty and pleasures of a wholesome sexually active relationship with a mutually chosen beloved partner.

This truce is vital to the future of humankind, its evolution and its species-perfection. Since young adults are tomorrows parents, teachers and leaders, a well rounded, balanced outlook on life by their tomorrows must be constructed this very day. It must be done in a manner that brings out the very best of themselves that they can be.

This book is neither about the encouragement of piety nor an exercise in obscenity, for I am not religious, neither am I hypocritical about anything. I do not play with words, and you will come across many which you may find *inappropriate*, but only seemingly so. Everything has a name and I will use those names generously. Case in point is that a vagina is called a vagina, and a penis is called a penis. Semen is called semen, just as spades are also called spades, not table spoons.

What I offer for your consideration is purely technical, not moral. Humankind's current moral standards are fickle and ever evolving or devolving with its mood. This is due to the lack of a solid basis upon which to determine what constitutes its morals or personal values. This book will also thus serve to teach you about the only basis that you will ever need for deciding what your morals or personal values should be.

The primary cause of sexual preoccupation of the obsessive sort manifest in humankind's experience is non other than sexual suppression, at the determinant stage of puberty.

I choose to use the term *suppression* in this book, as opposed to *repression* that has a dual meaning. It is important to leave no one in doubt by the end of the first read, that the overt brick-walling of young adults from wholesome sexual experiences and its ill effects, is the soul of this book.

Let us now work together to correct the idea of sex within the collective mind of humankind, so that it is seen as a gift to be enjoyed, and not a curse to be endured.

God himself loves sex, a lot

The true Nature of *God*

It has been said before that the simplest story may indeed be the hardest to tell. Everyone has their idea of *God*, others do not even acknowledge the existence of such a being. Yet it is true that all things must have originated from someone, something or somewhere.

A need then exists to correct the mass misconception about the idea of this being who created all things. A correct concept of *him*, *his* ways and processes is a necessary foundation upon which I will effort to heal the mind of you, the reader, from your preoccupation with sex because such preoccupation is the basis of many a sexual problem humankind is currently faced with.

Tell me, when last have you intently looked into the starry night sky? Breathtaking is it not? A person once inquired of me, after having humoured me in the reading of my many *insane* thoughts:

"where is *God* in the picture?"

That question is a truly pertinent one. Religion would say that *God* is everywhere. This is mere lip service because an objective being cannot be everywhere at once. At other times, religion would respond that *God* is in heaven, which then begs the question of where heaven is located.

Growing up a Christian—in the catholic church—as a child, I always imagined *God* to be a bearded King Arthur-looking individual, wearing a crown on his head and seated on a throne, with a sceptre in one hand. He had his needs met by numerous winged humanoids called angels, whose purpose of existence was to serve him for all eternity. He probably never stood up from his throne to go for a walk. The majority of you reading this have also been brought up in one organised religious setting or another, therefore if you have never thought anything similar to mine about *God* then please put your hand up.

This picture of *God* is false. Even addressing the idea of *God* as *God* or *a God* carries with it a lot of falsities about what *it* is not. It is quite difficult for most also, not to refer to *God* in the masculine, male sense. "He is God," most people always say.

Why is *God* a *he* and not a *she*? Why is *he* called *God* as opposed to being called *Goddess*? Ahh! One cannot say, "he is Goddess," for that would be grammatically incorrect. So if *he* is *God*, who then is *Goddess*? No *Goddess* exists, perhaps? The choice of the word *God* is thus problematic in and of itself and the sooner you drop it, the sooner will *its* true nature be obvious to you. The sooner also will your understanding of sex evolve to greater, truly enjoyable and wholesome heights.

For the sake of teaching you all this, I will label the idea represented by the word *God* as *the source of creation*. I will also use both terms interchangeably. I know it is quite a mouthful, but inappropriate or *convenient* labelling of ideas soon get lodged in your mind and it is not long before you begin to consider your own errors as truth. As we proceed with this book, the benefit of appropriate labelling will speak for itself.

The following may be new and strange to you, yet it is none the less a fact, and you will comprehend this truth for yourself in due course:

The source of creation is neither a *he* nor a *she* alone. *It* is literally, *both*.

It has no particular gender or sex, and yet it is a hermaphrodite. A hermaphrodite is genderless even while bearing both attributes of male and female. A true hermaphrodite is therefore a self-contained *procreater*.

Creation of the universe by the source of creation is a very, very sexual affair. It would not be able to pull it off as a *single dad* any more than your father could have fathered you alone, without your mother to assist in the process. The process of your conception as you now know, my dear young adults, was a very sexual affair. It was not the placing of your body into your mother's womb through the use of a magic wand or sceptre.

The source of creation, whom I will now further label *Nature* interchangeably, has not one set of rules for one affair and another set of rules for other affairs. Principles in Nature are universally applicable, always.

Creation through sexual union is a universal fact and is not limited to the human and animal kingdoms alone. It also equally applies to the vegetable kingdom, as it does to the mineral kingdom. Sexual intercourse, by any other name, as a means of creation is simply how the universe works.

In telling you of the hermaphroditic nature of the source of creation, I know you have already imagined within your mind, the picture of an objective, kingly individual—for those of you who are religious—who possesses both a vagina and a penis. You have also probably imagined that *in the beginning*, it inserted its penis into its vagina to create the universe. While that is quite *the picture*, if I do say so myself, it actually makes more sense than the creation of the universe by means of a magic wand or sceptre.

The idea of self-copulation is quite accurate actually, except for one fatal flaw. That flaw is that the source of creation is not an objective being. It does not possess two hands, two feet, a brained-head decorated with hair, a pair of eyes, nose, lips and so forth. It most definitely does not have an objective penis or vagina, but their working principle is the same as all things else. The idea of its *penis* and *vagina,* and how they work to create, is universally applicable.

The question naturally is that of what the source of creation looks like. It is with a simple question such as this, as well as others, that a simple story which is the answer, becomes the hardest to tell. It is hard to tell because of what you have been taught so far. May I advise that you do one thing throughout the duration of reading this book? Forget everything that you have ever been taught about the source of creation, till you are finished with this book. Keep your mind open, accepting nothing and rejecting nothing.

I will refrain from going into the exact science of the nature of the source of creation, for while it is something that you must come into knowing eventually, touching only on the rudimentary basis of that science will suffice for my needs and yours, where the purpose of this book is concerned.

To now properly answer the questions asked about *God*:

Question: "Where is *God* in the picture, especially in relation to sex?"
Answer: *God* is the whole picture—frame, canvas and image or images.

Question: "Where is heaven located?"
The whole frame—canvas with images—is heaven which is exactly what *God* itself is.

Question: "What does the source of creation look like?"
Answer: The source of creation looks exactly like what it is, the vast omnipresence of apparently black, vacuous space.

Again, in case you missed it, the source of creation is space. Yes, *it* is the cosmos itself within which all things have their being. When you look into the starry sky at night, always will you see two things. Bright lights and apparently black nothing.

That *black nothing*, space, is the source of all creation or *God* that humankind has debated since it first started wondering about the origin of itself and all things. The source of all creation really has no objective form, for it is mind alone. Space is exactly what your mind—one with the source of creation's—which has created and maintains your body, looks like. It is an invisible reality that manifests as the colour of nothing or black to our eyes, and as silence to our ears.

Within your own mind, you think and imagine. You visualise and even have your greatest, most elaborate sexual fantasies, my *teenage* Padawans, that would give an erotic novel a very, very good run for its money. It is exactly the same with the source of creation, for creation—the bright stars, planets, moons and all things else—is all an imagination happening within the mind of the source of creation, that space is.

Space is therefore hermaphroditic since it must possess male and female attributes which are mandatory to creating any form of creation. In other words, space is both the idea of a male and female at the same time, and I will give you simple analogies with which you may understand how this is so. The process of imagining an identity or thing into being is as a result of non other than sexual intercourse between the self-contained male and female aspects of the source of creation.

pleasured, but another be pleasured by you and vice-versa. The cupped hand does not *feel* anything sexually pleasurable, after all. Girls, your fingers are sexually indifferent to your vulva and vaginal stimulation, a penis is not. It takes a whole two... to tango, or so the saying goes. Do not worry about the source of creation's perceived loneliness, for it experiences and is well entertained through all created things, and equally shares in their pleasures as it does in their pain. All is one.

The Two Desires Of The Source Of Creation And The One Law Of Balance

The source of creation has only two basic but universal desires. The only acceptable currency of exchange between both desires is the *one law of balanced manifestation*. The desires are as follows:

1. The desire for action from expanded rest. The positive, polarising, male, action or penile principle.

2. The desire for rest from compressed action. The negative, depolarising, female, reaction or vaginal principle.

If these desires do not scream to you of "I LOVE SEXUAL INTERCOURSE" by the source of creation, then please tell me what else does. These two desires are the basis of much *sexual good,* with attempts at their violation, the basis of much *sexual bad* for humankind. In so saying, I do not speak of the objective, genitalia sexual intercourse alone, but also of all conceivable human affairs. The law of balanced manifestation between those two omnipresent desires always wins, because the male and female principles must always have their equal turn in all affairs.

In other words, the back and forth principle is omnipresent in all objective or subjective affairs under the *umbrella* of spacious cosmos within which all things have their being. Now let us look at examples of the back and forth principle, and what happens when attempts are made to deny each their equal manifestation in a manner that is timely:

1. From a state of rest, you awaken to conduct your daily affairs. The male principle.

After conducting your affairs of the day, you return to the state of rest in sleep. The female principle. You repeat the cycle.

An attempt to violate the law of balanced manifestation between both halves of the cycle is not an offence against the source of creation, but against yourself. For instance, you are to report to work by seven in the morning, but by three of that same morning you are still wide awake regardless of the reason. You manage to show up on time and all is well, or so it seems.

You failed to manifest the female half of the cycle

relative to the male half of the previous day. It becomes inevitable that your day will be as drowsy as it will be unpleasant. Your struggle to stay awake is the proof of victory by the one law of balanced, equal manifestation between male and female principles. The law of balance cannot be broken, it is that simple.

2. A young child still yet to master its body has gone to bed without emptying out its bladder. The female principle of the over expanded bladder's wall is an attempt to exceed its quota of expansion. Said in other words, the child is inadvertently attempting to violate the law of balance by denying its bladder the manifestation of the male or compressed principle.

The body continues to fill the bladder with fluid, further expanding the wall of the bladder beyond what it is designed to accommodate or is normal to it. The law of balance intervenes, but when the child is still in bed. It forces a manifestation of the male principle, by contracting the wall of the bladder to expel the fluid. You see, one can only *try* to exceed a balanced manifestation between male and female principles, but the law of balance always *butts in* to win the day. It has done so for the good of the child.

In a hypothetical scenario where the muscles of the bladder are made of the proverbial steel, balance will still win for an explosive decompression will occur, but the consequence may be a fatal one. It would not be punishment from *God*, it would be punishment of self in an attempt to break the law between the balanced manifestation of two desires, a law which is simply not breakable.

The law of balance between the ideas of compression and expansion remains un-debatable. It is universal and absolute, and there is no affair under the umbrella of the cosmos which is not either male or female in one sense or the other, such that it is bound to the law.

The back and forth principles relative to the law of balance equally applies to over expanding the stomach by filling it with more food or fluid in one single sitting than it is designed for, without allowing the collapsing, emptying-out half to be made manifest before refilling. It equally applies to the lungs as it does to the rectum.

3. For whatever reason, a person has not had food to eat for too long. The female principle of expanding the wall of the starved—that is, collapsed or compressed—stomach has not been manifested for too long. The male principle is simply being over manifested. The law of balance intervenes and all manner of discomforts arise; from your attention incessantly being drawn to the need of the stomach for expansion, to the stomach seeking relief from an overbearing male principle through the digestion or cannibalisation of itself in the form of ulcers and such.

The law of balance will do anything to get the wall of the stomach to open up, even if it has to destroy the stomach to do so, for the female principle, one way or the other, must have its equal turn at manifestation. It is nothing personal, it is just the way the universe has been designed to work. By filling the "empty" stomach with food, expanding it, the pleasure of release from compressed strain is instantaneous.

On the other hand, if such hunger has been due to a real lack of ability to obtain food to eat, as opposed to fasting, an individual may be sufficiently traumatised, in the psychological or mental sense, that over eating becomes a natural and balanced mental response *or reaction.* There is the fear that since the next meal is not guaranteed, eating as much as possible in one sitting is the wise thing to do, even though such fears may be unfounded in reality.

Anyone who fully understands the foregoing should already perceive how well I am building up my case against sexual suppression of young adults by parents, as well as its psychological consequences, as seen in the excesses of adult sexual behaviour, who simply cannot control themselves. It is a completely psychological or mental effect.

Returning to food, the result of such psychological counterbalancing by the law of balance is obesity. The law of balanced manifestation between the two desires of the source of creation, present in all affairs, is simply not breakable—physically or psychologically, objectively or subjectively—and humankind must understand this. Any attempt to break the law is immediately counterbalanced to restore balance, for better for worse.

Failure To Balance The Two Desires Is Self-Punishment

The very existence of back and forth needs or desires by your body, as well as pre-designed methods for the satiation of those needs is sexual intercourse, and the failure to equally manifest or balance both halves of the cycle is self-punishment.

The sleep-wake cycle is sexual intercourse. You punish yourself when both halves are not in balance.

The thirst-drink cycle is also sexual intercourse. You punish yourself when both halves are not in balance.

The drink-urinate cycle is sexual intercourse. You punish yourself when both halves are not in balance.

The hunger-feeding cycle is sexual intercourse. You punish yourself when both halves are not in balance.

The feeding-defecation cycle is sexual intercourse. You punish yourself when both halves are not in balance.

The inspiration-expiration cycle of the lungs is sexual intercourse. No one need tell you of the near instantaneous effects of an attempt at unbalancing that arrangement. Balance always wins.

The heart works through sexual intercourse between compression and expansion. Nobody can survive without the heart's sexual intercourse. We are all also familiar with the consequences of when one half of the heart's sexual cycle reigns supreme over another. Fatality eventually occurs to restore balance, of the permanent sort.

Moving a finger requires sexual intercourse because some muscle groups must relax from compressive tension, while another group must be made tense from a relaxed state, all in the bid to move the finger. I have no medical background and neither do I need one to know that the law of balance between compression and expansion principles works irrevocably, and is applicable to all affairs under the umbrella of the cosmos that the source of creation is. Do not worry if my case against sexual suppression of young adults is still not clear. We have many pages yet to be filled and I intend to be very frank about the situation.

You go to the store and collect what you need. You then go to the cashier and give an equivalent in cash. Everybody is happy. That is sexual intercourse, and because the exchange was balanced, you are always welcome to that store just as they are welcome to have your money.

May I offer a small challenge to you, to find one thing that is or can be done without sexual intercourse being involved. Send me an email. In the subject field, place the word "challenge" in capital letters in case you are still in doubt as to the universality and necessity of the principle of sexual intercourse, for anything to be or work.

There is indeed nothing at all that can be done

without a balanced exchange of condition between two sides of an *equation*. The source of creation has thus ordained that in all conceivable pairs of opposite transactions, all must add up to zero where both sides of an *equality sign* are concerned. Failure to do so will result in a forced attainment of zero or *fifty-fifty,* and as a young free-willed species prone to attempts at violation of the law of balance, the choice of that zero is thus humankind's alone, for better for worse.

The benefits to naturally manifested balance in any affair is as obvious as the personal inconveniences of forced attainment of balance. In the case of the transaction at the store, simply walking away without paying for what has been collected will be balanced by a visit to the nearest police station. Even then the equation still adds up to zero, one way or the other.

The source of creation therefore requires that all transactions between pairs of opposite conditions must be equal, they must be balanced, they must amount to *a zero* by the end of a cycle. The law of balanced manifestation is unbreakable. Only the self of one who tries to break the law will get broken, just as humankind is broken and keeps getting broken with regard to sex. It punishes itself needlessly.

Satiation Of Human Sexual Desires Is Not A Request

Let us apply the balance-sponsored back and forth principle as written to human sexual affairs, and test for validity as well as universal applicability.

Remember that the source of creation creates because it has two desires which I will again repeat here and in other words, so that it is lodged firmly within your mind:

1. The desire or need for tension from relief.

2. The desire or need for relief from tension.

Both desires must be manifested in equality or balance. They must be fifty-fifty, or add up to zero by the end of the cycle. All created things, from heavenly bodies to a grain of sand manifest the first desire of the source of creation. Their decay manifests the second desire of the source of creation. These two principles are omnipresent and repetitive or cyclical.

Sexually or reproductively speaking, humankind like most aspects of other kingdoms of life expression is not hermaphroditic. It has been sex-divided to embody one of the two sexual desires of the source of creation necessary to re-create or reproduce itself. It is however worthy of note to mention, that in all things else, humankind's physiology is patently hermaphroditic.

The male body through its penis is specifically designed to manifest the first desire—pleasurable compressive action from the idea of an expanded, relatively cold-blooded rest. While it eventually manifests the female pleasure principle through an ejaculation that slightly expands the closed urethra, dowsing tension with relatively cold semen after a sex-sponsored high temperature has been reached, the male desire remains supreme.

The female body through its vaginal canal is specifically designed to manifest the second desire—pleasurable expanded, vacuous rest from the idea of a compressed, relatively hot-blooded, tense action. While it eventually manifests the male pleasure principle through an orgasmic spasm that closes the vaginal canal, regenerating its lost heat after a sex-sponsored low temperature has been reached, the female desire remains supreme.

Males through their penis require pressure, temperature increase or a squeeze for pleasure. Females through their vaginal canal require release from pressure, temperature drop or to be *un-squeezed* for pleasure.

"Babes lemme *un-squeeze* you, please." Anybody?

It is perhaps necessary to state here that my thrust is not to explain the act of sexual intercourse within the context of its function merely as a tool for reproduction. My interest with this section is to give you an understanding of why sexual intercourse *is not a kind request* by the source of creation which may be accepted or declined on a whim, as parents do on behalf of young adults. Failure to wholesomely satisfy one of the two desires present in your body according to its sex, especially when such a desire is at its highest peak in puberty, leaves a psychological effect that only gets counterbalanced by an unhealthy preoccupation with sex as an adult. The law of balance finds us all, for better for worse.

Let us consider the penis more closely:

The outer diameter or girth of a fully erect penile shaft represents the idea of the source of creation's state of expanded rest, within which lies a raging desire to be compressed or polarised—the desire for action. The vaginal canal is specifically designed to fulfil this need.

By inserting the expanded penile shaft into the vaginal canal, it is squeezed or compressed most pleasurably. The repetition of inward and outward thrusts occurs until the desire for action from rest is fully satiated—the male principle. There is then the explosive reversal, at the point of seminal ejaculation, in which the desire for rest from action is made manifest—the female principle.

Let us now consider the vaginal canal more closely:

The closed state of the vaginal canal represents the idea of the source of creation's state of compressed action, within which lies a raging desire to be decompressed or depolarised—the desire for re-action. The expanded diameter of the penis is specifically designed to meet this need.

By cradling the expanded diameter of the penile shaft, the vaginal canal is released into an expanded state of rest. This release is deeply pleasurable. The repeated opening and closing through cradling and de-cradling of the diameter of the penile shaft continues until the desire for rest from action is fully satiated—the female principle. There is then, in some cases if not most, the implosive reversal of orgasmic spasms in which the desire for action from rest is made manifest—the male principle.

I could twist the words upside down, left-side right, and it would still lead to one conclusion. When it comes to the satiation of sexual desires built into the human body, Nature is simply not making a request for you to accept or decline. It is humankind's choice however, as to how dignified the satiation will be, and by taking a look around at the current state of human adult sexual affairs, it is choosing the undignified path through parental suppression of sexual activities in young adults.

Dignified Satiation Of Sexual Desires In *Teenagers* Is In

Humankind's Best Interest

The desire for sexual intercourse comes from the source of your being who is in and all around you, whose sexual nature is equally yours. The desire for sex is therefore dignified in nature, it is *Godly*. It is also holy, or is that wholly? It is intended to be experienced and enjoyed in dignity, with a mutually chosen and appropriate partner, if it is to have a lasting effect of the sort that prevents unhealthy preoccupation with it.

The need for sexual intercourse most certainly does not require the institution of marriage to be satisfied with dignity, any more than one needs to be institutionalised to have a drink of water or urinate same. *Fornication* is therefore a myth. Humankind will eventually learn to stop confusing the law of balance with its many man-made laws. Culture, tradition or legislation does not really make a thing legitimate, only the natural law of balanced manifestation between opposite pairs of conditions does.

Every individual has spent the first decade or so of life in sexual abstinence. This is one of the longest natural periods of abstinence from sexual activity all individuals will ever have in their active lives. When things work naturally, a young child not only abstains from sexual intercourse, it is too a large extent simply not interested in it, other than through transient curiosity, as well as whatever it is that mummy and daddy could be doing which requires a lot of moaning.

Today's deep sexual interest by children well too young to need copulation is testament to a generation of adults who simply are unable to get a grip on their sexual desires, due to no fault of theirs. The world is so sexually over-charged right now, only a very naive person will entertain the notion that young children are not watching and being unwholesomely affected by the counterbalancing discharge of adult sexual excesses. Those uncontrolled discharges turn back inwards to sexually overload children who left to natural circumstances, would be too young to seriously care about such matters in the first place.

When it comes to the sexual needs of young adults—that we arbitrarily label teenagers, who have just emerged from roughly a decade of ideally natural sexual abstinence—the directive of "thou shall abstain" is simply unnatural and cannot truly be abided, nor should it be demanded of them. It constitutes a monumental psychological and physiological affront of the highest magnitude, an insult against the sanctity of natural *creater-endowed* sexual desires and their satiation in a manner that is dignified.

Such a demand for abstinence is never without counterbalancing consequences, and very much analogous to the psychological consequence of severe food starvation that leads to obesity when food is finally and easily obtainable. Telling sexually ready young adults that the one severely heightened desire that they badly need satiated after about a decade or so of abstinence, is the particular one that may not be satisfied is also a major factor in the battle of egos between parents and their young adults. It is actually a case of hidden transferred aggression resulting from sexual suppression. Young adults unknowingly resolve that they are not the only ones who get to be denied what they desire—rebellious behaviour becomes the name of the game.

May I suggest all parents with young adults be about pondering the foregoing very carefully, to see how it may apply. May I also suggest parents with children who will soon enter the stage of puberty start drawing up a plan to at the very least attain the semblance of a win-win situation, so that your children remain yours in heart and mind, and not *cousin itchy-slippery-finger's* personal brothel, which you may never hear about to be upset about, unless of course blissful ignorance makes for a better night's sleep.

Beyond legitimate concerns of premature pregnancies or the transmission of diseases which is easily prevented through education and the encouragement of unpunished transparency in the sexual activities of young adults, there really is no excuse parents have for denying young adults the dignified satiation of their sexual desires, to nip sexual obesity as adults in the bud in very, very good time.

...or is it not your responsibility to raise the next generation of adults? What then are you parents for, because someone said you had to?

The consequences of ill-advised decisions to launch radioactive ballistic missiles of penalties against young adults who only desire what is natural, births fully grown adults who treat their sex lives as if they stole the permission to have sex from their parents— adults who simply have no sense of restraint or self-control whatsoever. Fully grown men of today are obsessed with their *collection of Barbie dolls,* and fully grown women their *fleet of teddy bears*. These are effects created by parents who, sadly, are still very much *inside the heads* of their now fully adult children, without the awareness of the latter. The mind can be a funny thing sometimes.

Sex by adults of today is mostly just a mechanistic affair and no different from compulsive eating on a full stomach that stems from an insidious psychological trauma associated with unnatural and unnecessary abstinence, undignified or *stolen* sexual encounters as young adults. Is that how we would much rather have things be? Indeed it appears we do, for the law of balance is finding humankind where sex is concerned, and in troubling ways, which really need not be so.

The satiation of sexual desires is a biological imperative born of the two desires of the source of creation present in all affairs, and does not readily make itself available to anyone's philosophical, moral or ethical opinion to the contrary. The satiation of all desires in wholesome ways is a purely technical, lawful concern and not a moral one. An environment must therefore be created to meet needs in ways which do no harm to self, another or the whole.

Humankind through its religions, cultures or

traditions has not been sincere enough to ask itself the question of why it is that every single biological need of the human body is readily catered to, from when they first manifest, except the sexual one. No ones seeks another's permission to go to sleep, quench thirst, fill a hungry stomach, empty out the bladder and rectum. The heart most certainly does not need anyone's permission to function. Yet these are all manifestations of sexual intercourse and the law of balance relative to them which says, "meet these needs through provided avenues, or they will be forcibly met. It is nothing personal."

There is absolutely no real need to fear the wholesome, dignified satiation of sexual desires in young adults, so much so that we suppress them. It is one of the main ways by which prevalent sexual issues will be evolved out of the human experience, as humankind continues its journey towards perfection. Where ever do you suppose the presence of mind to rape another comes from? This question is better answered by another. Why do you suppose people steal food to eat or water to drink?

By the way, is it not yet time we redefined what constitutes puberty? You see, humankind presumes the onset of puberty—more obvious in girls as menstruation—to be the beginning of sexual development. Is it? I would beg to disagree. Try this perspective on for size and see how you feel about it:

1. From sexual conception to birth is the baby developmental stage. Birth marks its end.

2. From birth to the first sign or evidence of sexual reproductive capacity ought to be labelled the stage of puberty. The evidence of reproductive capacity should mark the end of puberty, not its beginning. A girl child can easily become pregnant roughly coincident to her first ovulation. In other words, if she perchance had sex then, all would be suddenly greeted one morning by a certain pregnant someone who supposedly has not even *reached* the stage of puberty. Is that a commencement of sexual capacity development, or is that a completion? Just a thought for you to ponder, dear parents.

3. From the end of puberty—per my paradigm, of course—to whatever arbitrary age in which one may be pronounced an adult, should be labelled *adult or mental developmental stage*—the young adult stage. In this stage the mind and body catch up with already matured reproductive organs.

4. The end of the young adult stage—which humankind has arbitrarily pegged at eighteen years of age—till death marks the adult stage. This is a stage in which an individual should be mentally matured, most especially with regard to sex.

You do not agree? Well then, let us have a look at what happens, when parents gloss over the first and second stages which are essentially the offices of physical and reproductive capacity building.

Still going by my paradigm:

1 and 2. We treat the *pubescents* like complete imbeciles, all googly-eyed and clown-faced, basking in

the novelty and halo of parenthood. We even throw in a few episodes of *Teletubbies* or similar ill-advised entertainment, to make sure children *get the message* that they are *cuter* when they behave like complete imbeciles. My apologies, but this is true.

3. We then treat the young adults, parent-capable as they are, like pubescents and wonder why no one can get along.

4. Young adults treated like pubescents throughout their mental developmental or young adult stage, are then suddenly told that they are adults because their age says so, whereas they have just psychologically entered the young adult stage. Basking in their new-found sexual liberty, they go overboard with it. These ones are our today's adults and parents, who are actually young adults masquerading as fully mentally matured adults.

An advanced age sets in with the arrival of true mental-adulthood, and young adults all the while masquerading as adults finally come into wisdom, having binged on sex so much so that their unbalanced sexual appetites is counterbalanced by a sudden drop of interest in sex. They can no longer have children and the behavioural wisdom whose value they now realise is lost to the next generation, because those ones simply do not wish to hear it. It becomes a simple case of "you've lived yours, now lemme live mine." Would it not be wonderful is such elderly individuals were actually parents of young children? Young adults under them may turn out to become more sexually level-headed under the guidance of the elderly, once declared adults. "May," says the author.

In making the error of treating young, reproduction-capable adults like pubescents—per my paradigm—who do not really know what they need, humankind merely defers a whole mental developmental stage from when it should naturally occur, to the stage of when they should be wise, level-headed parents who can keep their families together, and their genitalia firmly in their underwear. By denying young adults any form of respect whatsoever, they grow into adults who simply do not or cannot respect themselves. The cycle repeats.

When all else fails, as if that is not what is already happening, do consider that I could be terribly mistaken. That is okay, for the task of seeking workable solutions should not be mine alone. Let everyone therefore put on their thinking hats, rather than let me or anyone else do the thinking for you. I do not run a church, after all.

Dear parents, the young adults will become married parents in a decade or even less. The natural and wholesome control of sexual desires which they dearly need to be ideal parents is not something to be learnt as parents. Learning such self-control in a marriage is the reason why many marriages fail, and families are needlessly torn apart. It is because sexually charged young adults parading themselves as mentally matured adults have been entrusted with a commitment that they are anything but ready for. The ideal time to "get it over with" is as young adults, not as adults, much less married parents. The overbearing parental policy of sexual suppression, so-called protection, of young adults is therefore terribly misplaced.

As a species we need to help the young adults get their perspectives on sex right, so that it stops being the basis of many catastrophic decision making processes as adults. Right now, sexual favours is the currency of exchange in many facets of human adult society, or is that young adult society? A young lady here in Nigeria for instance, can barely get through school without being sexually blackmailed by her professor or lecturer who may be old enough to be her grand father, or probably has a daughter her age. She can hardly get a job unless she satisfies someone's sexual needs. Conversely, women use sex as a tool of control and manipulation of men.

Sex, sex, sex! The shenanigans being played by humankind around sex is as tragic as it is hopelessly amusing. The source of creation indeed has a very... well, *curious* sense of humour, for want of a better expression.

The Suppression Of Sex Is The Root Of Most "evil"

The Water World And The *Common* Table Salt Parable

Out there somewhere in the far reaches of the universe, orbits about a sun a rather curious planet. With the exception of a lone continent, its entire surface is covered in normally salty sea water. The inhabitants of this world are relatively prosperous and have all their lawful needs met with ease and dignity, except one. *Common* table salt.

It so happens that the inhabitants of this planet have agreed, or so it seems, to have a wall built around the entire continent. It serves to prevent access to the sea because the collective believes that salt is too enjoyable to be for everyone, most especially anyone under a predetermined age. However, all other citizens of this continent may experience the enjoyable taste of *common* table salt only when obtained by officially sanctioned and often stressful means. Acquisition of salt by means other than what has been sanctioned is considered theft and frowned upon.

The enjoyable taste of *common* table salt therefore is one of the most expensive or difficult-to-experience treats anyone can have. Everyone loves it but all have been essentially starved of it. In fact, the degree to which common table salt is loved is so deep, that it is an object of unhealthy obsession.

Two young adults, a boy and a girl, where recently apprehended by the law keepers and severely punished. Their crime? Breaking into a closed store in the middle of the night to steal common table salt. The store into which they broke stocked a variety of items for sale; from jewellery made of pure gold, the latest gadgets, to food items. These teenagers could have easily taken any of these items and probably gotten away scot-free, but they did not. They just had to go for the *common* table salt, the one thing everyone has their eyes on.

Young adults or teenagers are especially placed under constant surveillance in their society, for they cannot be trusted around *common* table salt. They are therefore not allowed into stores which sell *common* table salt. Should they arrive at such stores with their parents, they are required to remain outside unless they can produce a valid identification that places them at or above the prescribed recommended age limit for *common* table salt consumption.

Parents take extreme measures to make sure that their young adults never have access to *common* table salt. The *common* table salt in the home is stored underneath the bed of the parents, and their children must never witness when their parents partake of it.

Parents send their children to guarded boarding schools to ensure that they never gain access to *common* table salt. The unfortunate truth is that such an environment is where common table salt is abundant, but not in its purest form. Parents like to pretend that such is not an issue.

The young adult population happen to be at a biological stage where the sensitivity of their taste buds to *common* table salt is extremely heightened, and yet it is the one thing they may not have with dignity. Meanwhile, they are also bombarded on television screens by entertainment programmes which focus on *common* table salt.

The adults have set up a whole paradigm of entertainment centred by *common* table salt. They call it pay-per-view adult *common* table salt or *salto-graphy*. The *common*-table-salt-needy young adults, tech-savvy as they are, have unbridled access to salto-graphy. They have no choice but to live off of it as an alternative, till the day that they are *officially* allowed to partake of the taste of *common* table salt.

When the young adults finally reach the minimum required official age, as if a bird released from a cage, they flap their wings in the endless pursuit of *common* table salt, and never stop flapping unless they fall out of the sky in *exhaustion*. They simply cannot get enough of it. They binge on it, obsess over it, sell it and buy it. Even while married and *entitled* to *common* table salt, they still seek out other avenues to obtain same, to the detriment of their family. Having become parents, the cycle thus repeats itself.

A man came back home unexpectedly to meet his wife giving a portion of the couple's jar of *common* table salt to their neighbour. The portion being given was no much more than a tea spoon full. In a burst of uncontrollable passion, the man reached for his revolver and shot dead his neighbour, wife and then himself, over... *common* table salt.

A grown up man was walking down a poorly lit street one night. He prior to then considered himself an upstanding member of society and had no history of inappropriate behaviour. Walking towards him but from the opposite direction was a lovely young woman whom he observed to be nibbling on a popular brand of very *expensive* biscuits, called *salty snaps*.

He looked around for signs of anyone who could bear witness, or indeed intervene in what he suddenly intended for this young woman. She had barely walked past him than he suddenly turned back around, reaching for her mouth to silence her scream for help.

What did he desire from her? Her salty snaps. He took the biscuits forcefully from her and ran off into the poorly lit night, leaving behind an emotionally traumatised woman who may just have willingly shared her salty snaps with him, if he had just asked politely.

I could go on and on, but sincerely, have you ever heard or read of anything more confounding or insipid? Or have you?

One may think this hypothetical scenario as being far fetched, but is it? The fact that a people for whom salt, common table salt, is just about the most abundant thing in their whole world—being completely encircled by a salt laden body of water—would *choose* to deny themselves of it, is truly a phenomenon worth a standing ovation. In choosing by hook or crook to make salt hard to get, these people have ignorantly sowed the seeds of inordinate preoccupation with salt.

If you replace salt in this parable with sexual intercourse, then adjust more specifically for context, it becomes obvious how utterly ridiculous and silly our ideas or generally accepted beliefs about sexual intercourse truly is. Humankind, needless to say, possesses an enormous baggage of issues about sex, a needles problem identical in principle to the self-created *salty needs* of that rather curious water world.

On our world there is hardly a person who is not adequately or naturally equipped with at least a penis or a vagina. These body parts are so well designed to interact with each other in such a way that the mutual pleasure derived is so exquisite, so glorious, so enjoyable, so satisfying. The thought that such an amazing experience is so easily accessible is why in our ignorance, we have created about it, a *great wall*, and decided what grouping of humankind may partake of the pleasures found on the other side of that wall. Each generation of humankind attempts to exclude the part of itself, young adults, which needs sexual intercourse the most.

The Reality On Ground

The idea as represented by the saying, "that which is resisted persists," is a universal truth and the basis of sexual issues which keep self-repeating or persisting from one generation to the next. For those of you who are able to comprehend, my short science book, "*Thermodynamic Laws Versus Universal Law,*" is a recommended read on this matter, because sexually related challenges experienced by humankind will keep repeating—being perpetual in motion—till a new seed is sown in humankind's consciousness that enables the manifestation of adults who are in effortless control of their sexual desires.

Parents of each succeeding generation carry on in blissful ignorance and self-satisfaction that they have the entirety of life all figured out. While it is to a large extent true that parents' life experiences contain much which a child can learn from, the sad fact is that each succeeding generation is still consistent with the attitude of repeating the *failed ways* of the preceding generation in most affairs of life; from politics—a presumed form of leadership, to religion and science, culture and traditions, and yes, managing the sexual desires of young adults.

I once met an individual, an elderly man actually, who once told me something that I could not help but respectfully acknowledge and further ponder because of the simple truth it represented, at least within the context of our conversation. He said to me, "you may have more new clothes than I do, but my old rags are still more in number than yours." His demeanour was one of a person well accustomed to having his words of sound advice cast aside, wisdom that would do a lot of good being imparted to young adults as they grow *mental feathers* rather than when already in *flight* as adults. It would be a matter of negligence to fail to acknowledge the value of life experiences of our elderly members of society, for they contain much wisdom on many a concern which one could easily learn from to avoid repeating needless mistakes already made by them.

While that is taken into consideration, there is still need to question some aspects of wisdom because sometimes I wonder if they actually *got the point* themselves about sex, and I am very desirous of giving them as much credit as is due them. However when something does not work, it simply does not work. Humankind is currently drowning in its own misfired sexual excretions, and so far there has been no real proposal nor sound words of advice to correct the trend once and for all. Misplaced abstinence is a causal factor, not a solution.

Legislation is not the answer either. It only addresses the effects and prescribes punishment for sexual acts which are arbitrarily deemed *illegal* based only on opinion. It is helpless to tackle the presence of mind in people to choose unwholesome sexual behaviour. Psychology cannot be legislated, but it can be adjusted and evolved with the knowledge of truths of existence.

Humankind's laws are only effective to the extent that individuals are actually caught, then proved guilty of acts deemed illegal. It implies that as long as a person is not caught or can arm-twist human legal systems like most do, such one is okay. Such delusions do not help anyone, it most certainly does not help the human species in general. For every jaw dropping sexual misdeed that is publicised, I wager that there are at least a hundred thousand more that no one will ever hear about.

Parents, fathers especially, throw a fit when they discover that their young adult daughters are having sexual relations with boys of their choice. All hell breaks loose. Meanwhile, some fathers are having sexual relations with their own daughters. I personally find this amusing because the question I naturally ask myself is, "which then is which?"

We all hear such news of the latter and everyone goes up in arms—"kill the bastard! Kill the bastard!" Oh come now dear ones, have you not any idea whatsoever how common incest is? Of fathers having their way with their daughters... and even sons? Then it will also shock you to know that most children never speak up because they may be, well, *enjoying it*, far much more than they are afraid to report the abuse. This is not judgement upon anyone, I am merely saying what is so. This is all happening in a world where parents blatantly refuse or raise a holy hell over any form of dignified sexual activity by their young adult children. Now tell me, who exactly is fooling whom?

The fact remains that with or without the approval and guidance of parents, the young adults are having copious amounts of sex, as they actually should, but the problem is that most times it is occurring in ways that are neither dignified nor beneficial to their general outlook on life as adults, who will in due course also become parents.

The lack of logic behind sexually suppressive wisdom by parents in general has never been obvious for the strong message being passed on to the next generation of adults, that they may choose all manner of less-than-ideal sexual behaviour, but make sure not to get caught. The tangled web weaved by such innocent ignorance becomes even more entangled, from one generation to the next.

Let us now translate portions of the water world parable into the reality on ground that we may see for ourselves, if it is not already obvious to you, how humankind's current methods of sexual desire management in young adults not only not works, but also sows very unfortunate seeds which will end up being passed on to their children when they too become parents.

Pornography

Oh dear! If you have never looked at pornographic content, please put your hand up.

Have you ever asked yourself the question of why pornography exists in the first place? Humankind seems not to know that like in the case of the bladder becoming so full or the stomach so compressed in emptiness to the point that they become hazardous to health, pornography hazardously manifests the law of balance because attempts are constantly made on behalf of young adults to violate a balanced manifestation of one of the two creater-endowed desires built into their bodies.

You see, sexual suppression—so called abstinence forcefully demanded of young adults—is like filling a balloon with gas or fluid beyond what it can tolerate and expecting it not to explode. A violent explosive decompression equal in intensity to the degree in which the normal condition of a balloon was exceeded is an outworking of the natural law of balance. Pornography is that explosive decompression which renders that *balloon* unusable in the way it was originally intended.

Remember that the source of creation within whom we have our being has two desires. The desire for compression from expansion, and the desire for expansion from compression. Both conditions must have an equal or **balanced** share in their manifestation, and one can never cheat the other even though it may appear successful at it for a time.

If compression holds ground for seventy percent of one cycle, expansion will be fine with the remaining thirty percent, but its manifestation will be as spectacular as it will be memorable. It will express with such radioactivity, that supporters of any arrangement that is unequal, unbalanced or less than fifty-fifty ought to remember the folly of such mindset of trying to be *smart* or economical with certain truths.

Generation after generation, humankind refuses to give room for the dignified satisfaction of the creater endowed sexual desires in its young adults, and rather than give room for such, it prefers to legislate the radioactive effects of the lack of dignified desire satiation in adults. Today one of the effects of sexual suppression, homosexuality, is contending with nature on its right to be regarded as a family unit for the purpose of raising the next generation of humankind, to teach them what?

Some countries have made it legal for same sex individuals to be married essentially for the purpose of being a family unit with respect to the raising of children, rather than creating a system that allows young adult male and female couples to enjoy their intimate company with grace and dignity, without an intention to raise children.

Lack of a sense of priority as to the appropriate application of legislation is the reason why anyone needs to legislate same sex marriage in the first place, with a view to letting same raise the next generation of the human stock. Humankind as it is cannot even handle what is naturally intended, how then do homosexual parents intend to handle what is not naturally intended? What exactly is presumed will be the overall result on the next generation of adults?

The next section will be on homosexuality. Please understand that I do not sit in judgement nor do I have an opinion about any of these matters that may be considered moral or otherwise in nature—I have long ceased that behaviour. My considerations are purely technical and aim to point out what simply *does not work* relative to what we claim is desired as a free-willed species.

It is necessary to briefly tell you about my personal history with pornography. It becomes necessary to do so to jar you out of any false impression that makes me *holier than thou*. I too, one way or the other, am a victim of current methods of sexual desire management of young adults, and have suffered the ill effects of preoccupation with sex as an adult. I do however pride myself in asking simple pertinent questions. There is no more powerful a question that one can ask on any matter than the *why* of it.

Towards the end of my junior secondary school, I discovered pornography. Oh what joy! Can you imagine the feeling? Cloud nine! I chanced upon a *business transaction* among my classmates which dealt in video cassette tapes, the microSD cards of my era. One of us was a very astute businessman, who every other week, supplied pornographic videos and magazines to anyone who was willing to part with a small sum to keep the *treasures* for a week.

What else was I supposed to do? I must have been twelve or thirteen years of age and all I could think of was sex, sex, sex. My society had made me *scared* of girls such that I felt as though I would be branded a serial killer of sorts, should I do the unthinkable of asking a particular girl whom I silently loved dearly for sex, much less actually *do it*. Her father was a wealthy man and she had a lot of very fierce looking brothers, who could probably snap my neck with a very focused, telekinetic glance.

My home was without a father and filled with women who were *useless* to advise me, and my only brother who might have *shown me the way* had left the country for greener pastures, as most Nigerian youth typically do. The situation was hopeless and my desire for sex, much less with the one I loved and daydreamed all day about--who probably did not even know that I existed by the way—would never be met. This is the world we live in. This is the world in which young adults are expected to manage romantic and sexual desires *the best way* they can, except of course, partake of sexual intercourse.

Who can therefore judge me, or anyone else, for choices of behaviour which served to create a semblance of balance in my system? Pornography was my answer and even when I ponder it in retrospect, I simply have no regrets because *it is what it is.* It helped immensely in my sex-urge management, which could not have been done any other way. Full stop.

Religion is hopeless to truly address the issue of pornography. As a matter of fact, it is one of the prime contributors, in a disturbingly reverse-sense, to the *importance* of pornography in people's lives. Religion spreads its generally sexually repressive mental tentacles, by working through parents to suppress sexual desires in young adults.

Young adults in general would much rather skip visits to guilt-tripping religious houses when left to their own devices, it is parents who compel them there. Growing up in the Catholic church, we were taught that Jesus was conceived by an immaculate conception, and over a billion faithfuls actually believe that. What a mountain-sized load of rubbish. It is truly amazing to what depths the Vatican in particular sinks to make out of sexual intercourse, a very dirty deed. Yes, I just judged, and I stand my ground against religion in its current form.

Rather than tell the world that Jesus was conceived through the normal means of a sincere love-borne vaginal penetration by Mary's partner, Joseph, they invest time and effort to make a case for sex being such a no-no, unless such couples are institutionalised in a ceremonial marriage of their approval. These sorts of false projections about sex by religion always made me feel guilty about my sexual desires, and by the time I concluded that I had had enough, I was already neck-deep in pornography. One cannot simply guilt-trip a person for feeling hungry. If a person does not acquire food in a dignified manner, much sooner rather than later, such a person will *steal* it. That *theft* is exactly what pornography is. Natural needs must be met or they will be met with, *for better for worse.*

Much as I do not regret my utilisation of pornography together with masturbation to satisfy my sexual desires, I will readily admit that my outlook on life from there onwards was a complete and utter disaster. A few short years later, the internet was introduced and it took my *mastery* of pornographic content to a whole new level. When I later realised the effects that it was having and decided that it was not okay with me, it took a great deal of willpower and effort to reverse the mental damage.

My first sexual experience was extremely and regrettably late, and somewhere in my mid twenties when I like most would supposedly be considered an adult fit to be a parent, if finances will allow. I recall it from memory with much difficulty so as to place here in writing, for it is one that disturbs me till this day. I did nothing *bad* actually, but then as it does now, I feel as though it did not represent the highest idea of myself.

Having subsisted on pornography throughout my young adult years, it became natural that I would seek to emulate what I had imprinted upon my mind. Also I had no way of knowing that apparently, virgin males experience a *wee* bit of a challenge in their first penetration of a woman, and it was nothing to be really worried about as to ability, unless of course such male jumps into it, like I did, feeling like a *Super Porn Star,* to his humbling embarrassment.

If that fact is not universally applicable, then I am very happy to call it my personal challenge at penetration for the first time. It was a lady friend of mine with whom I was recently sexually involved that *educated* me on that *little bit* about virgin males being nearly useless at sex their first time, as I narrated my... *traumatising* ordeal to her.

Still on my *first time*, I was so shocked at what seemed to be my inability to do the one thing I had dreamed of my whole life, infecting my mind with all manner of media from the internet in the process. I then had a *bright idea* that my partner give me an oral sex, which she willingly did, if that was what it took to get the *holy business* under way, because I simply was not getting anything done with her.

Now I speak for myself in saying that not only did I not like the oral sex, which she was very, very good at by the way, I simply could not shake off the feeling that I had just insulted her dignity regardless of her personal opinion on the matter. My technical consideration here was very simple: if I did not see myself giving her oral sex, out of fear for this or that, why then should I have asked it of her? That did not feel right to me, and I suppose one could say that I have always had an intuitive understanding of the law of balance well before I started investigating it.

I will end the story by saying that my

pornography-sponsored exercise in passionless mechanistic buffoonery, did not end well. Not only did I not feel good about the experience or adequately satisfy my sex partner, we never spoke again for other unrelated reasons which we were both fine with. There is a very, very big difference between pornography and sexual intercourse undertaken in mutual respect and reverence between partners, and I do not mean marriage. With caution do I say the following then:

Majority of humankind is only having pornographic sex—mutual masturbation—not real sexual intercourse.

Now in case you are thinking that this is some sort of a confession or an attempt at an abridged sexual autobiography, "please don't." It is merely much easier to make my point using myself as an example where it applies, because I am not interested in sitting in judgement of individuals. I merely wish to state, to the best of my knowledge, what does not work and why.

Everyone has or will have their own personal experiences which is always a private matter not to be pried into, but the point remains that the problems faced with regard to sex is a general issue, and not an individual one. Let us therefore refrain from hypocritical, bigoted attitudes and work together sincerely to cure the species of its sexual maladies.

In my time as a young adult, there were no cell phones and the fixed landlines worked only on occasions. Today we have broadband internet and wide screen, ultra high definition smart phones which cost just about nothing. In most countries, only young adults who live under a rock do not possess access to the internet through these devices.

In my time, when the internet was introduced, computers could be secured with appropriate software to filter out pornographic content. Even then, a simple *control-alt-delete* or an exclusion of the censor software from the next boot-up sequence took care of that little nuisance. Today you dare not touch the computing devices of young adults. You can try, but it will most likely be locked behind many layers of security specifically designed to keep everyone out.

I shudder at the thought of what the current generation of young adults is doing with pornography, and how severely injurious to their outlook on life as adults it will be. If the trend is not counterbalanced, not by way of force or judgement, but by sowing new seeds of more enlightened perspectives and behaviour, humankind *will* devolve, irrecoverably.

Parents, please read very closely. I have opened my internet browser and have typed in a single word, "nude." I have selected the "image" tab and made sure that all filtering is removed to give me the... *best results*. Let me talk you through what I am looking at on the thumbnail images which show up. I am compelled to be very graphic here for the sake of some of you well intended parents who are living in a fantasy world about what young adults, the adults and parents of tomorrow, have to go through because humankind through you sexually suppresses them.

The first image on the first row of images is that of a woman, naked of course, with her legs spread apart and her cervix exposed through the use of a speculum.

A few rows down is an image of a man inserting two fingers into the anus of a woman.

Towards the bottom of that page is a woman being mounted from behind and her vagina penetrated, by a dog. In case you missed that, I just said, a dog. Pets in your home, anybody?

The search term used is relatively *sterile*. Now I have typed in a more *direct* query, "porn." The more impactful results on the image tab are as follows:

A woman is having sex with two men. She therefore has one penis inserted into her vagina and the other into her anus.

Further down a man inserts his hand, up to his wrist, into the vagina of a woman.

There is a woman here performing oral sex, and has semen dripping out of her two nostrils.

Two naked men are passionately kissing each other, with one behind the other. Very ironic, because this same passion is always missing in pornographic content between men and women. Could it be that the seemingly headless pornography industry also has its own agenda, in addition to satisfying sexual desires? A thought to ponder.

There is an image of a human-sized sex toy—head, neck, arms and legs removed—complete with a gaping vagina. It appears that the anus is also available for utilisation, considering its size.

Two men in the shower kissing, with one groping the chest of the other as if a breast.

Now this one is *very interesting.* A woman displays a portion of her rectal wall, having successfully turned it inside-out. It is protruding through her anus. A money shot?

Would you consider me a disrespectful or vulgar person in making you read all of the above? If you do, then indeed you have your ahead buried in the sand. The pornography industry exists to fulfil a need, the very one that humankind denies is in need of being fulfilled in a timely and dignified manner just as equal in importance to hunger, thirst or the evacuation of fluid and solid waste from the body.

Not very many people go to the internet to seek media of others sleeping, masticating food, drinking water, urinating or defecating. The fact that very few people seek these sorts of media is why no industry has been made out of them. Those needs are met most times with a fair amount of dignity. No one therefore preoccupies themselves with such.

Widely suppressed sexual needs however have a very successful industry created to meet those needs. Thus it is that Nature cannot be cheated, but we can cheat ourselves in so attempting. The law of balance is unbreakable and attempts to break it are immediately rebalanced or counterbalanced. One merely has to decide if the manifested balance is what is desired, because the source of creation has no sense of morals. It is not human and has no need for such, nor a need to hurt or injure anyone in punishment because there is simply nothing humankind can do to hurt or injure it, but humankind can hurt or injure itself in punishment and indeed does so in many dramatic ways.

Humankind is sexually self-injured both due to ignorance of the law as well as breathtaking hypocrisy. When you deny your body the dignified rest of sleep it needs, sleep will locate you at the most inopportune and undignified of time. When humankind suppresses its *creater*-endowed sexual desires, those desires locate it in the most potentially damaging way.

Which then will it be, dear parents? Are you all going to rethink your current strategies, or are you going to continue with the status quo and let your innocent children become exposed to things which will only hurt them, as well as the whole human species that will shortly be under their care?

Returning to the love of my life back in secondary school. Assuming that I had summoned up enough courage to talk to her and she perhaps loved me back, would it have killed anyone or cause an apocalyptic-level event to share and enjoy a loving, intimate, bonding sexual union with each other? Could we not have been sex mates, enjoying each other's company in grace and dignity after taking necessary measures to avoid an unintended pregnancy? Who would it have hurt, really?

Is the foregoing not preferable to my many mental developmental years with pornographic content as mine, and most certainly her mental food? Would a declaration of our mutual love and sex partnership to the full awareness of our parents not have instilled upon both of us, a sense of responsibility?

Do you parents have any idea whatsoever how much time young adults waste in pre-occupation with sex and pornography, which can be used more productively in study or other worthy pursuits? What do you suppose the world would be like if every single adult was balanced and level-headed, having very quickly moved past the phase of intense sexual curiosity, becoming wise in their adult years rather than waiting till an elderly age to exude wisdom and sexual temperance belatedly, or when society is no longer interested in their input?

Can you now understand that humankind has got everything backwards, that what it thinks it is doing to protect its younger population is achieving *everything but that*? What we resist persists, what we look at critically, goes away. It is time to take a very close, critical look at current sexual desire management strategies in young adults for *they simply do not work*.

LGBT

Before I go into the LGBT or homosexual subject within the context of sexual suppression of young adults, it is important to state that there are many other reasons why people choose this style of life. It is my hope that on the glorious day that organised science overcomes its materialism, it will do some proving objectively, such that there is no longer left a shadow of doubt as to what a majority-cause of LGBT predispositions may be.

One of my favourite authors, Dolores Cannon, spent her life doing something that really needs to become mainstream, with regard to the diagnosis and treatment of many a human concern. She specialised in hypnotherapy of the sort that successfully uncovered the source and solutions to problems of her clients, by accessing their personal history across previous lifetimes. She published many books containing reports from her sessions. They are indeed revelatory, and very much worth a read by all.

LGBT issues in most cases do not originate in the present life time. In some cases it will be discovered that an individual, for instance, may have spent perhaps one too many life times incarnate as a male. They then find themselves in the body of a female, and much as the memory of previous life times is not present on the surface, it is deeply imprinted as a habit on what is labelled the subconscious mind, and becomes the basis of predispositions as well as sexual choices or decision making processes. Such an individual having been as a male for too long struggles to find comfort in the body of a female, and retains a sexual perspective towards other females that is the office of a male.

It equally applies to individuals who have spent too many life times incarnate as a female. In being as a male in a current life time, such individuals retain a habitual sexual perspective towards males that is the office of a female. In countries where the general population is more liberal or indifferent to the LGBT situation, some individuals go as far as the use of hormones and surgeries to re-enforce their internal protest against wearing the wrong gender *meat bag*.

It is most unfortunate that religion has proved utterly useless in the true spiritual enlightenment of humankind, and instead adopts a bigoted stand on the matter. If religion knew anything about the truths of existence or the law of balance which always seeks out every affair to create a balanced situation, it would work to let most struggling LGBT individuals know that it is okay to be in the body that they are wearing, even though they are uncomfortable with it. It would let them know that the task of this life, among others, is to manifest a balanced or appropriate perspective relative to the gender of the body being worn.

It would teach how to be comfortable in what ever gender is manifested at inception and how to represent and savour that gender's attributes as faithfully as possible, and to be content with it. It would also teach, when all else fails, that they may wait till the end of their current lives and then take a more preferred body or gender in a next life time, in preparation for another try at embodiment of an opposite sex in subsequent life times. One will find that in such a case, the individual becomes well acclimatised to that gender manifestation by the end of that life time, which was the original pre-incarnation intent in the first place.

Some of you may be wondering about my interchanging use of gender with sex. I saw a documentary about a very, very popular American transgender teenager, in which he—per his actual reproductive biology—made a case for distinguishing the idea of gender from sex. He argued that his body is one, but his *brain* the other.

Now I mean no offence, but I have to be brutally honest here. This is merely a case of semantics—word play. The human species is patently sex-divided relative to its reproductive functions, and unless he is genitally hermaphroditic, as inter-sex people are, he can only be one or the other, not both. True sexual hermaphroditism is only achieved in sex-divided species through sexual intercourse with an opposite mate.

I think it would be much easier on him if someone just told him that he merely does not like wearing a male body—that souls are sexless or hermaphroditic and may manifest as either gender in an incarnation— and that there is therefore really no need to be subconsciously addicted to one sex or gender alone.

...but who will do the telling, when religion or

other factors such as entertainment are hard at work, and practically successful, with their absurdities.

I conjecture, considering the very tender age in which he rebelled against his body, that this individual has spent too many life times as a female. Regressive hypnotherapy or even so much as a mere surface awareness of the reality of his personal pre-birth history, will help him understand the source of his grief and heal his wounded heart, so that he may move on with his life as a young man.

Religion is instead interested in teaching its absurd hell fire theories that only work to drive away people in need of enlightened—not bigoted—advice. Many individuals simply cannot comprehend their sexual attraction to the same sex and are helpless to even so much as guess that in most cases, it does not stem from the current life time. Most fear to talk about it to someone lest they be attacked. They then spiral downwards, deep into despair and suffering.

Humankind indeed has much truth to be taught and the task of doing so is daunting, I must confess. The LGBT matter is simply not being handled in the best way possible. Punitive legislations in some countries such as Nigeria simply do not work, because they ignorantly treat effect and are utterly hopeless to address the cause. What such laws only say is that, "don't get caught, otherwise, *as you were*." Legislations which encourage LGBT styles of life are no better either, for they are only prolonging individuals' learning process, needlessly deferring lessons from this life into the next.

When it comes to bigotry, it is always an amusing sight to behold the reactions of self-proclaimed homophobes, when their children come out as being LGBT individuals. The law of balance simply respects no one, as what expands outwards as bigotry and judgement eventually turns back centre-wards as a memorable *personal experience*, with the lesson being that all issues are collective issues, not individual or isolated ones.

This planet is a very peculiar one in her service to humankind as a school of learning, where as many life times are allowed as is necessary for each person to sort out their personal baggage and attain perfection from the experience. In one of my last life times I was very critical of human choices of behaviour that I disagreed with. In this life time, the law of balance has caught up with me and I am experiencing what I did to others. It is not punishment, it is merely the perfection of my soul through the learning of what works and what does not work.

In a previous life time I was very critical of drug addicts and cigarette smokers, as well as LGBT individuals. In this life time I struggle with an addiction to cigarette smoking, and I am constantly thought of and harassed as a homosexual individual due to my apparently effeminate physiology, by even complete strangers who know utterly nothing about me enough to possess such preconceived notions in the first place.

Do you suppose that those *strangers* are really *complete strangers* in a universe where all is one? I may very well decide that I choose to be a homosexual individual, but you see, it would not be because of my physiology, the one thing over which I have no control. Can you imagine how disconcerting and infuriating it is for a woman that I would like to date, to ask if I am gay? Ouch!

I must have been about ten years of age in this current life when I looked straight into the eyes of a young and sweet innocent girl and asked her if she was a witch. The look of horror which emanated from her face in response to my question is still very clear in my mind, and *haunts* me to this day. I very much wish that I can meet her someday and tell her how so very sorry I am, not because I now realise the folly of that action, but because it does not represent the highest idea of myself to cause harm to another especially through the careless use of words, and words can be very, very destructive.

Having been brought up in a superstitious and heavily religious environment, I *assumed* the little girl's generally calm, quiet, self-respecting demeanour and what I then considered to be her ragged clothing the basis of my conclusion, that something was *wrong* with her. What you project from yourself dear readers, eventually locates you. Please beware.

Truly what goes around does come back around and all must be careful about seeds being ignorantly sowed, for if they do not germinate in this life time, they will do so in the next when you have no memory of having sowed such seeds, and therefore the least prepared to understand the lessons being given to you.

The reality of previous incarnations is behind the many seemingly unusual events in people's lives. It is also the answer to the question of why apparently *bad* things happen to apparently *good* people. There is no good or bad from the perspective of the source of creation as all actions or decisions are eventually balanced, fifty-fifty, for the sake of soul evolution. Such evolution simply cannot be achieved in one flimsy life time alone. The science of this is to a large extent present in my other book on the idea of perpetual or repeating motion, and its universality in all affairs.

Let us now return to LGBT affairs within the context of sexual suppression in young adults. Causes are not entirely related to past life history alone, they are also caused by enabling environment. I have heard a saying go that, "in the absence of the desirable, the available becomes desirable." This statement is correct, for it is another way of saying that the law of balanced manifestation between the two desires of the source of creation will always win, and say with me now... *for better for worse*.

In some cases where young adults lack the means to satisfy sexual desires, the environment may *step in* to present an *available* avenue for satiation of such desires. The existence of pornography becomes even more problematic because it does not delineate sexual tastes. If you seek pornography you will get it, all of it, including the LGBT as well as other *creative* sorts.

I once watched a documentary film centred by

the LGBT subject in which I believe it was a professor who made a very interesting comment, that we indeed live in a very homo-social society. The reality is more conspicuous in African as well as other nations which are ultraconservative about the subject of even so much as normal *teenage* sexual experiences, much less LGBT ones.

I have personally always questioned the wisdom of same sex schools, particularly the boarding schools. The professor in that interview vocalised my thoughts in his use of that simple and very succinct term, *homo-social society*. The extent to which parents of young adults go to protect them from the *dangers* of dignified sexual experiences is extremely detrimental to the highest good of the human species, and I am of the opinion that same sex schools should no longer be entertained because they have no benefit whatsoever.

It is an exercise in hypocrisy, futility and self-deception for parents to think that placing their young adults into same sex schools or boarding schools at the height of their greatest need for sex serves as a reasonable means of protecting them from themselves. I wonder if such parents have never heard of cases of cannibalism of dead human bodies being completely necessary to the survival of those who remain alive after a terrible event, and that in such extreme cases, the *cannibals* cannot be blamed regardless of how truly disturbing the idea of cannibalism is.

What makes such parents think that sexual desires cannot just as well be satisfied with members of the same sex? In males, this can be particularly problematic because the anus and rectum are simply not designed to be treated in such a pumped manner, nor to be ejaculated in. In females, homosexuality is technically benign because they have no organ with which to penetrate the vagina, unless an artificial object is utilised.

A story was narrated to me by an old friend—who attended a boarding school for a while until his parents *grew wiser*—of a case in which a senior secondary school boy compelled a junior to perform an oral sex on him. They were caught and all hell broke loose, or did it? Would you like to guess how many more similar cases in the entire history of that school have occurred, was occurring, will occur, and will never be found out? Have parents really any idea whatsoever how common sodomy is in all-boys schools? To think otherwise regardless of available statistics, is like saying that boys do not get hungry or thirsty when huddled together under one roof, for extended periods.

What do you suppose was or is the psychological effect on both individuals, and what sort of adults or parents do you suppose they will become, especially with the younger boy having been subjected to such humiliation from his senior in addition to both of them then being paraded before the whole school, severely punished and expelled? Was corporeal punishment and expulsion the solution? Who created that environment? Who sent those boys to that environment? Who denied those boys the means of a wholesome or dignified satiation of their raging sexual desires? Who exactly is fooling whom?

In some societies like Nigeria's, boys are only to be seem with boys. Girls are only to be seen with girls. Sirens go blaring and eye brows gain in excessive altitude should there be a deviation to that formula. This is enforced under the guise of wisdom, experience, culture and tradition. I personally find the irony of it all very amusing. Is it preferred then that boys and girls go into an LGBT style of life as opposed to a sound, loving, intimate relationship with a mutually chosen member of the opposite sex? Which then is which, because abstinence from sex is as impossible as abstinence from the need for food or a drink. Abstinence may be physically enforced, but the venomous effects are very long term.

In boys this manifests as the expression that "every hole's a fair goal," and it matters not if that hole is the cup of the hand, a hole in an un-sliced loaf of bread or the anus of another boy, or even girl. Should that behaviour imprint through repetition, it becomes a way of life and such an individual proceeds to label himself *homosexual*. It is very important to harp on sodomy because the faecal system can experience severe damage when used as a vagina. This is a purely technical consideration, not a moral one.

Again, Nature has no sense of morals because that is the office of self-determining free-will creatures. Nature has however done its duty by adequate provision for the satiation of all needs, because that is its parental nature. The use of such means for any activity other than designed is not a question of morals, it is a question of upsetting balance which simply cannot be upset. Anal fissures present in men and women who practice sodomy is an example of the law of balance working irrevocably.

If Nature—the source of creation—was interested in the opinion of morals, it would have made predators vegetarian so that they do not prey upon seemingly helpless animals. However, the law of balance being absolute will see to it that the body of predators become fertiliser for their vegetarian prey, who are therefore not-so-vegetarian themselves after all. The law of balance therefore is not a moral concept, it is a purely technical one.

Humankind is expected to have a sense of morals or values, but they should be based on the one law and not on fear, misinformed opinion or bigotry. All must know *the why* of a thing not being workable and not just have fickle opinion about it, most times inherited from others. What remains true however, is that LGBT affairs in the long run and for the sake of the species simply needs to be evolved out of the human experience, but in the most enlightened way possible.

LGBT matters present with the species in most cases is empowered to persist, because the young adults must have their sex, one way or the other. Boys must have their penises *squeezed* outside-in, and girls must have their vaginas *un-squeezed* inside-out. Why not let these natural desires be met with dignity? It will do no damage I assure you, but instead create an opinion in the minds of young adults about sex— extremely absent in current adults, by the way—that is healthy, beneficial and to the greater good of the human species.

Rape

I once watched a documentary film about a supposedly primitive nomadic tribe in the forests of the Amazon. They are the most amazing group of people I have come to be aware of. They live their lives entirely in the nude.

It is inspiring to watch the interactions of their men and women. It is completely innocent and very clean-minded. The population of children running about indicates that the adults are not ignorant to the divine pleasures of sex. It is not vocalised in the film, but the young adults must also be engaged in sexual activity, because their carriage is so balanced, and the demeanour of the young adult boys and girls so level-headed, even in the presence of their mutual nudity.

There is no way that a twelve to fourteen year old boy is not sexually aroused by a nude girl of the same age and vice-versa. Unless they are made of logs of wood, such self-control has not come to be through abstinence, but dignified sexual interactions. I could be wrong though, or am I?

The narrator further revealed that all birth-capable women in the population partake of a certain plant that suppresses their menstrual cycle. They only take the antidote when there is a deliberate intent to conceive a child.

There is therefore little to no reason not to conclude that this is a very sex-loving group of people, or they would not be using contraceptives. They are not hypocritical about sex neither are they preoccupied with it, any more than they would bother to be preoccupied with eating food, when the forest gives to their balanced ways most abundantly. What chances are there then that rape exists in this small society? I wager zero to none.

How many of you young adult boys of today as well as grown men, or even fathers, can stand the sight of a nude woman without being sexually aroused? I most certainly know I cannot. Oh wait, do you think me a log of wood? Am I not also the product of *the young adult sexual suppression system?* I after all did not grow up on the moon, *neither did you.* Humankind's lack of sexual self-control is therefore a general issue, not an individual one. Why do you suppose a man would force himself sexually, upon a woman? Where does the presence of mind to do so come from? People convince themselves that rapists are "bad people." Are they?

Let me tell you a story about a near-rape sex encounter I once had in school. I and a couple of friends went to the night club as we usually did every other weekend. It was a relatively productive night, for we came home with *good catch*. Or so I thought. I later realised at the end that the lady who spent the night in my bed had no choice in so doing because she lived far away and the driver of her group was not leaving our accommodation without a good round of sex, or two, with her date.

I had no reason to doubt that I was going to have some *freaky sex* that night and *thanked the heavens* for this rare and wonderful occasion. Well bathed, naked and prepared, I jumped unto the bed to get down to business, but she was not interested. "What!" I thought to myself.

I was convinced that it had to be a joke or perhaps her idea of foreplay—I have once met a girl who likes *more than a bit* of force with her pleasure. I proceeded to *insist*. I kid you not in saying that the situation rapidly degenerated into a case of rape. I was so shocked when I realised it. We did however *not* have sex, as I had a deep impression to back off, even though feeling sorely disappointed and very sexually frustrated.

From where do you suppose came my presence of mind to sexually harass that lady as I did? The answer is suppression, sexual suppression as a young adult which left an indelible mark on my mind as an adult, as well as an unwholesome perspective on sex through use of pornography. Here is a lady I had just met, and I assumed that I had the right to have sex with her because she found herself in my room.

If my first exposure to sex in life was one of undiluted love, affection and mutual respect rather than pornography, would I have had a need to go to a night club in the first place to bring home a complete stranger and demand sex of her, simply because I bought her a few drinks? Could she not have easily reported me to the police? Would I not be labelled a rapist and a sex offender, whether pre-meditated or otherwise?

You see, we continue with the business of deluding ourselves as a species that sexual issues of all stripes are isolated cases, or merely only of bad people doing bad things. I would not have believed it, if anyone foresaw and warned me that I would have a probable case of date-rape on my hands before dawn. Humankind's sexual issues are not individual, they are collective. What I mean by that is that we have inadvertently created an environment in our ignorance of the law of balance, that predisposes us to all manner of sexual behaviour.

People do not normally go to the store to steal food stuff that they can easily pay for. Take away that ability to pay for food, and you may have a case of shop-lifting. The urge of the food-starved person to counterbalance the empty stomach through filling it with food is the law. The action of a hungry stomach was counterbalanced, unfortunately, by a reaction in shop-lifting. Since reactions also become their own actions, a new reaction of being taken away to the police station is inevitable.

In the shop-lifting scenario, not once was the law of balance violated, but the balance created was of the undesirable sort relative to the shop lifter, who may have chosen to seek better avenues to meet the need of hunger satiation. So it is too with rape. It is irrelevant if one chooses to label rapists by any name, but the human species is reaping the fruits of its own ignorant, hypocritical sexually suppressive sowing.

I do apologise if you were expecting me to pass judgement on anyone with regard to rape or other manifestations of unwholesome satiation of sexual desires. It is in making sure that I am not sitting in judgement of another that I have used myself as case in point. It is left to you all to ponder for yourselves how the rape scenario may equally apply to you, or how you are predisposed to it without even being aware of it. The presence of mind in adults to force one's sexual desire upon another is today being sown as seeds through sex suppression systems.

What we can do however is bring up the next generation of adults and parents in the way that they should grow and in the case of sex, resisting it on their behalf is not the answer. It is in letting their sexual desires be satisfied with grace and dignity, so that they may *get it over with,* that we will find the answer to manifesting sexually balanced adults.

In other news

I once saw a sex video taken of young adults in one of the classrooms of a private secondary school. The girl whom I estimate to be between twelve and fourteen years of age had two boys all to herself as sex partners, and she simply did not care that their activities were being recorded. Her body language as she mounted and cradled one of the boys, was one of intense sexual starvation. I felt a deep sense of empathy for her because for the boys, as we are indirectly taught by society, it was merely a glorious conquest.

I am always amused at the reactions and comments by people to *leaked* situations such as these. With all due respect to these commenters you really do not know what you are talking about, because such comments are based on the notion that this is an isolated case, and it rarely occurs. For this scenario which so happened to be recorded, there are many others that will never be seen, known or heard of.

Parents in particular grimace at the thought or sight of such realities, and speak in many foreign languages about how *terribly frightening* such things are. Newsflash: The young adults are having sex with each other all the time whenever there is an opportunity, even if that opportunity is injurious to them. To them the need for parents' approval is as irrelevant as the need for an approval to urinate, especially when the *bladder* is *full* to capacity.

Do you suppose that if this girl was allowed a

dignified sexual relationship with a mutually chosen partner, that this sort of event would have occurred? Would the parents of the children have to sit and watch their own having an orgy on the internet? What do you suppose as a parent that a solution to these kinds of events happening could be? Huff and puff? Single sex boarding schools? So be it.

I once came across an article here in Nigeria of a teenage girl publicly humiliated and then arrested, by the parents of a boy child over whom she was tasked to care for in their absence. The young adult girl had been having sexual relations with the very young boy, or at least had him masturbate her vulva. Her photograph was pasted all over the internet and commenters had their way with unbridled projections of all manner of intense criticism.

The answer she gave to interviewers on the *why* of the deed was as truthful and honest, as it was soulfully touching to me. She said in other words, that she had carried the burden [sic] of sexual frustration for so long, and not knowing what to do resorted to have the little boy *assist* her.

Here in Nigeria and probably other parts of Africa, we have an uncanny habit of going into the villages and bringing into the cities, young adult boys and girls to care for our children, as domestic house helps. These boys and girls are torn away from their families and friends where they are loved and respected, to come and babysit families with children that are sometimes the same age as they are. Most of them are not even given an education during their time of service with their very lives and future. They lack a choice in the matter because financial poverty is so deep, that any means by which extra income may be obtained is readily welcomed by their financially impoverished families.

In the case of the article just mentioned, we have here a young adult at the peak of need for sex satiation, who simply has no dignified avenue by means of which she may meet those needs. Whatever else would have become a most likely outcome, other than what she did? Would it have happened if she had a more wholesome way of meeting her sexual needs? Is her abstinence not the very root of that catastrophic decision?

Another way, not any better, in which she could have met those needs would have to become the secret number two wife of the *man of the house* because that is exactly what happens in many cases, going by reports of female domestic house helps suddenly sent packing, and of marriages falling apart from thence.

Now the list of issues is not exhaustive, obviously, but I hope you finally understand my point with regard to the folly of suppression of sexual activities in young adults. I could go on, but this is intended to be a short read, and enough has already been written to make the point clear.

The Religious Connection. Caution—Strong Words Of Criticism

It would be remiss of me to bring this chapter to an end without at least properly *naming fingers and pointing names,* as a certain *pirate* once put it. Religion is always guilt-tripping its followers about the general degeneracy of humankind's sexual behaviour, reminding them of how they were born by and in sexual sin, and how they must stay pure and free of the *sin* that sex supposedly is.

Organised religion is a very powerful and terribly mischievous force to be reckoned with. Its faith is based upon mere opinion or belief, not universal facts of Nature. Faith is a conviction that does not easily lend itself to any form of reasoning which does not agree with it. Where belief—upon which faith is based—is in error, then religion becomes a cause of many a problem. Just about the whole world population of humans subscribe to one mainstream religion or the other. They adopt their theological theories as their own, without any question whatsoever as to their validity or universal applicability.

It is left for you the individual to turn your eyes inward to your own organised religion so as to determine for yourself what about it works or simply does not work, with regard to sex and indeed many other concerns. I cannot do this for you because we live in a world so deeply charged by religious sentiment, and it is not my intention to pick out religions that are especially problematic lest I overly offend individuals, for which I have nothing to gain in so doing. I will only go as far as saying that religion, in general, is dead wrong about *God*. My proof of this claim rests in their mutual objectification of *God*, more so as a *he*. This is on one hand.

Please go out into a clear night and breathe in the star-filled sky. Everything you see out there represents the idea of children, and space is their sexless or dual-sexed parent. Said in other words, the stars and all things else are creations of their source that space— *God*—is. If you are part of a religion that objectifies space, then that religion is a valid candidate for a critical look-over, for it most likely has a teaching about sex that is anything but true.

On the other hand, since I have a Catholic Christian origin, it is to that origin that I will limit my more critical remarks. I simply choose to retain my right of criticism of that into which I was born, as it does not constitute an attempt at violating the rights of others to whatever denomination of Christianity or religion they please. I will speak about the Vatican's fatal short comings and its prime role in contorting the beauty, sanctity and universality of the idea of sexual intercourse.

The Vatican has only a faint understanding of the true Nature of *God*. Its doctrines are nothing but insults which constitute the ejaculation of semen straight unto the *face of God*, *its* ways and processes. I apologise in the announcement, that what little truth the Vatican has about the source of creation is merely superficial, with just about as much depth as a spit on a side walk.

In most cases, its most high priests do not really believe in what they teach. It is merely a profession for them, whose task is the mental enslavement of a whole species through sexually *repressive* doctrines, among others, that only work in the reverse sense to encourage sexual issues. They know full well that once people find out that they really have no *sin* to confess, and that penance or reaction is always self-contained within an attempted action to "offend" *God*, that they will be immediately rendered extinct. Do you think modern doctors—no offence—will have an income if and when people suddenly grow healthier? Let me tell you, your coming into knowing about the true nature of *God* is very, very bad for the Vatican's *business*.

The Vatican's not-so-covert war against the sanctity and universality of sexual intercourse—the war against *God* itself is a tale as old as time. Their efforts have been near well successful, and by their fruits *ye* ought to know them. One of their fruits, glossed over by more than a billion Catholics, as a minor technicality, is that its priests may never *be* with a woman as a condition of supposed service to *God*. This reality alone, smacks on even a dignified sexual relationship as being vulgar.

That in itself is really what is vulgar, not sexual intercourse, much less women. All things created come into being through sexual intercourse; from the elements, vegetables, animals, humans, planets to suns. All things are maintained by sexual intercourse. Sexual intercourse is the heart beat of the universe and without it, nothing except the source of creation could be. Why tell a man who only just desires to serve his fellow humans that he may not partake of sexual intercourse, so as to be like Jesus? Whoever told them that Jesus never had sex, and in copious amounts? What then is a priest—sexually suppressed as a young adult—supposed to do when the inevitable sexual urge comes knocking for balance? Say a novena, perhaps two? Sodomise an alter boy? Oh come now...

To you sincere Catholics who have been looking for the Antichrist or Anti-*God*, I am afraid you have been running a marathon with your eyes wide shut my dear friends, for the anti-true-nature-of-*God* is the Vatican. I therefore offer you knowledge of the law of balance as the only basis required to draft your personal moral values. It is the only law you will ever need. All the ten commandments are in that one law. Everything that matters to you is contained in that one law. The law of balance between pairs of opposite conditions is absolute. The very soul of those two opposite conditions is a male and a female, that is, sexual intercourse.

The idea of the supposed immaculate conception of Mary is perhaps still the greatest insult of them all, in the Vatican's centuries old campaign against *God*. Now I do not know about you, but I was most certainly not conceived or born in sin despite the Vatican's claims. My body is not a product of rape of my mother and if it were, that would be my father's problem, not mine.

I consider it a *sin* however, If ever there was such a thing, to insult the sexual conception of my body by calling it a sin, and then ask that I be baptised to wash my soul of that *sin* so that I am not condemned to *hell fire*. Oh dear! Can you imagine? The length and breath of effort taken by the Vatican to crucify the dual-sexed nature of *God* manifested through all pairs of affairs, including the pair that conceived my body, does not get any more vulgar than that.

I have asked this question on several occasions to get people really thinking, and each time I get the response of a blank stare, reserved for people supposedly as insane as myself. If *God* the father is male and *God* the son male, what sex then is the holy spirit? No one need strain to have the answer, because the Vatican simply never tolerates females within its ranks. The holy spirit is therefore male, at least according to the Vatican's self-evident masculine paradigms.

No one has firmly pressed the question as to why it appears that *God,* according to the Vatican, feels such deep *disgust* towards women, and then sex. Some Catholics would gun down an LGBT individual if they could get away with it and still go to *heaven*, yet they have never wondered about the patently sodomite nature of the *creative trio*, as implied by the Vatican's misinterpretation of the trinity idea.

Let me assist sincere Catholics on that one,

although you should already have the answer by now. The truth of the holy trinity—or is that the *wholly trinity*—in reality is as follows:

"*God*" the Mother-Father or Sexless or Hermaphrodite or C*reater*. AKA the Vatican's *God* the father.

"*God*" the Father or Creator. AKA the Vatican's *God* the son.

"*God*" the Mother or Creatress. AKA the Vatican's *God* the holy spirit.

"*God*" the Mother-father is neither the Father or Mother alone—*It* is **both**, hence the idea of the holy trinity, because it takes the union of the two to manifest the third, which is their source. Two lovers of the opposite sex coming together in sexual union is a manifestation of the source of creation in the fullest and truest sense, and nothing, my dear readers, gets holier than that.

Please let us move along, there is still yet ground to cover.

The Vatican also claims that reference to *God* as a *he* does not really mean that it is a he. Oh? Have we not language for ideas that are not masculine? Why not then call it a she? Ahh! That would validate the importance of women as well as sexual intercourse, which those in the Vatican cannot bare to stand, or at least pretend not to.

Let none therefore deceive you into making out

of sexual intercourse, the *evil* or fornication that it is not, to the point that you yourself do the putting of *evil* into it. Sexual intercourse is your right. It is yours to experience and enjoy. It is not the office alone of physical procreation. It is also the office of mental procreation, in celebration of life.

Let the young adults whose bodies scream of sexual readiness be allowed a partner and have sex as much as is desired, but let them be taught to do so in grace, dignity and mutual respect for one another as that is the only *requirement*, if ever parents are in need of one.

Young adults absolutely do not have to be made to treat sex as if they stole it.

Conclusion

Truce And The Way Forward

This chapter initially presented a bit of a challenge of the sort that made me wonder if perhaps I had not bitten off a whole lot more than I could chew, in the writing of this book. I had written this chapter, deleted it, and rewritten it several times. On one hand I realised this chapter's inevitable outcome, if I failed to change my approach, as a how-to for parents on the raising of their young adults. On the other hand, it would constitute my giving the young adults a how-to on compelling their parents to remember that they too were once young adults, and should therefore understand their need for dignified sexual experiences, with their opposite mates.

I could still go ahead and write two how-to sections, one for parents and one for young adults. Doing a quick internet search, the sheer volume of published materials for both parents and young adults on the subject of handling sexual intercourse affairs probably exceeds a life time's worth of reading, if nothing else was done each day. There is therefore no need to repeat them, even in other words.

Furthermore, any attempt to write a how-to would only be the case of just another e-book author who wishes to tell people what to think, especially since he himself is not yet a parent. I would much rather invest my time and effort in giving from myself to others, what I feel is necessary for them to think for themselves.

In any case, this book has picked out one of humankind's myriad problems, sex, and identified its enabling cause or causes. That in itself should suffice to get all, parents and young adults alike, to lay down their weapons in a truce, sit down on opposite sides of the dialogue table and chart *the way forward* in such a way that every body wins. Parents get to be parents, and young adults get to be young adults, complete with their much needed wholesome and dignified sexual experiences. The persistent generational war between parents and young adults is comparable to two very powerful elephants locked in a battle for supremacy. None ever comes out on top, but the grass upon which they tussle, humankind, always bares the brunt.

Let us then very briefly, recap the main points:

1. Humankind has an unhealthy preoccupation with sex, which leads to all sorts of choices that only cause harm to itself.

2. This preoccupation is a general problem, not an individual one. No one can sit by a corner and say, "look at them, dirty creatures," any more than one's body can feel indifferent to a stubbed toe. The pain from a stubbed toe reverberates through every cell in the body, and the entire body gets affected by the pain. Equally, humankind is the body, and individuals are each cell of that body. A stubbed toe in humankind's

body, that sexual excesses is, is therefore each individual's problem, together.

3. The preoccupation with sexual intercourse exists because humankind believes it is doing something wrong when it experiences and enjoys its sexual encounters. A very funny thing, the human mind, because it gravitates more excessively to what it is told it may not have, cannot have, is not good for it, will make it sad, will make it fat, or is deemed wrong, especially when such things have a pleasure-factor attached to them.

4. Such *warped beliefs* exist because humankind is rarely taught about the true nature of the source of all creation. Humankind has not been told that this bodiless individual within whose mind we all have our being, is the most sexually active person in existence. In being dis-informed about its true sexual intercourse loving nature, dressing it in a man-made garb of mentally injurious sanctimonious piety, item number three on this list manifests. Humankind, thinking that the source of creation is some sort of sexual virgin, views its sexual activities as an undignified form of pleasure, and treats it accordingly.

5. Feeling guilty about how so wonderful sexual intercourse is to the point of needless obsession with it, humankind attempts to play holier-than-thou with its children, the young adults, who are now capable of reproduction, and therefore sexual intercourse. It then wonders why parents and young adults are never able to get along. The young adults are forced to experience

the pleasures of sexual intercourse only through *"stealing"* it, that is, partaking of it without the knowledge of their parents and in ways that are undignified and unwholesome. This mental imprint carries on into adulthood. The cycle then repeats itself, through their children.

As you can see, this cycle has to be broken, and broken now! Since the law of balanced manifestation between all pairs of opposite conditions is unbreakable, a way around then, is to create a new, more enlightened action whose reaction will be more in accordance with what is desired. That is why I have written this book, to call for a truce between parents and their young adults, who will become the parents of *tomorrow*. I have placed within the pages of this book, the tools required to move past all forms of dis-informed thinking, and with which to draw up new personal values, moral standards, and living philosophy.

Let us recap what constitutes those tools:

1. Knowledge of the true nature of the source of all creation and its only two desires, the very idea of males and females, as well as the one law of balance governing those two desires.

2. I really hate to disappoint you, but there is nothing else.

If I will give any final words of advice on the exclusion of sexual suppression and its ill effects from the human experience, it will be in the form of two words:

1. Dignity.

2. Transparency.

There is no need to expatiate on them, instead, what I have done is write a short fiction. I have deliberately set it in an *apparently* far-fetched environment, because environmental or social circumstances for all individuals are not the same on this world. A short fiction makes for a much better way for each pair of parents and their young adults to draw up conclusions or solutions for themselves, that is realistic and applicable to personal circumstances. You must think for yourselves, using the *fiction* story, what can be done better in your personal reality.

Thank you for your attention so far, and I hope you enjoy and learn from what follows.

The End – A new beginning.

Andon And Lao – Fiction

Let me tell you about the culture of a civilisation in a far, far away land called Telos.

Planet Telos, a blue-green world which exposes its continents to the crisp fresh air of an oxygen rich atmosphere, is inhabited by some five hundred million people. Its continents when viewed from space register a deep green with patches of white, looking as though it is winter in a hot mid-summer.

In addition to their three main continents, to which smaller isolated ones are administratively attached, Telosians have constructed a floating artificial one, the capital continent called Q*uarters*. Quarters comprises a group of four perfectly circular islands, equal in diameter. Three of the four islands are arranged to form an equilateral triangle centred by a central island, and permanently interconnected to each other by six bridges. Each of the three bounding islands is used as the capital city for three representatives, *reps*, from each of the three main continents of Telos. The three reps together are referred to as the high council. The high council conducts the business of planetary administration from the central island of Quarters.

Today is officially the last day of Andon's childhood. It has been a whole twelve years of growth and development, as well as being indoctrinated into the ways of his people. Tomorrow is his thirteenth birthday. Andon and four other boys will be undergoing their coming of age initiation ceremony tomorrow, having been born on the same day. Telosians do not treat their children like play toys, whose early lives are merely for the cheerful amusement of their parents, and a lot of effort is invested in their upbringing. This allows Telosian children come into a high degree of mental maturity and a sense of self-responsibility, very quickly.

Andon is proud of himself, for he will finally be regarded as a contributor to society, and not just a boy. He also gets to follow in his mother's footsteps, for the next seven years at the great *space tuber* design and maintenance facility, as an apprentice systems engineer. At the end of his apprenticeship, he will receive permission to join in on long-term away missions to 5.0 level planets and below.

One of the benefits of coming of age, which excites him the most, is that he finally gets to *know* the love of his life, Lao, and it has been worth the patient wait. In forty seven years time—if still remaining partners—they will be permitted to undergo the ceremony of parental commitment, and then be placed on the high council's waiting list to conceive a child of their own. Since Telosians have a very long life span, they prefer to wait till they have acquired as much personal experience as possible, before embarking upon the task of child raising. Birth of a child on Telos is considered a serious as well as a sacred event, and treated with all reverence.

The Telosian main staple is laced with a contraceptive extracted from a certain genetically modified herb, which is grown in isolation to prevent unintentional access by wildlife. The widespread casual use of contraceptives in this manner was agreed to, through a planet-wide referendum several millennia ago, and is still agreed to after further review by each succeeding generation. Since they have long conquered diseases, unscheduled pregnancies which upset the balance of the human population is their only concern. The contraceptive culture enables them enjoy sexual activities with their partners, without concerns about pregnancy.

Life is beautiful on Telos, a 9.2 level planet out of the highest rating of 9.9 levels, which could easily be called heaven. Telosians do not use any form of money, are highly spiritual, and possess a prodigious understanding of the true laws of creation, such that their technology is as simple and discreet, as it is extremely advanced. Telosians are loved throughout the universe for their expertise and dedication to planetary evacuations of low level planets, in times of extinction-level natural disasters.

They also dedicate themselves to keeping preemptive watch over the nuclear shenanigans of low level planets, to prevent them from destroying themselves. Radioactivity is the only circumstance that threatens their ability and willingness to carry out a mass evacuation, should it become necessary. In one unfortunate incident on a level 2.9 planet called earth, in the city of Chernoblia, the local scientists lost control of their nuclear power plant in a radioactive thermal runaway.

Two engineers, based on a cloaked Telosian star tuber—a cigar shaped starship—stationed in orbit around earth, who were on nuclear patrol duty were the closest and first to respond. They arrived at the scene to render assistance. They were relatively late however, because the situation had rapidly degenerated beyond what the equipment on board their pod was designed to handle, but their immediate intervention was absolutely necessary to prevent the need for a mass evacuation of the planet. Earth's people were not in the least aware that they were not alone in the universe, and very likely to respond poorly to open *off-world* assistance, on such short notice.

The two engineers managed to extract the radioactive core and evacuate it from the planet using their pod. This selfless act however, cost them their lives as their pod's electric field did not suffice to shield them from such close proximity to the highly radioactive material that they had in tow. They died a very painful death in deep space, having been severely irradiated, but not before they saved the entire planet. Andon was only eight years old when this occurred, for his mother was one of the two engineers. He has ever since harboured ambitions of being stationed, long-term, in earth's system where his mother died a hero, and his.

It is dawn and Andon suits up for the coming of

age ceremony. He is wearing a very simple one-piece, long-sleeved, high and round neckline uniform. This one is made of a vinyl-like material, with a subtle surface finish similar to the bark of a tree, and immaculate white in colour. The clothing's trousers blend into his footwear which resembles a boot, but with a tight-fitted minimalist appearance. Around his waist is attached a utility belt made out of a thick strip of metal consistent with the appearance of a stabilised gold and mercury alloy, with no apparent point of attachment or detachment. To Andon's upper left arm is an emblem of a foetus still inside its womb.

"You bear a striking resemblance to me at your age, my boy," remarks Neldon, as he walks up to Andon holding a white robe in his hand. "Your mother would be so proud of you."

"Ouma, P'pa," replies Andon, embracing his father with much enthusiasm.

"Ouma, son. Here, let me help you with this," holding the oversized robe out to Andon, so that he can slip into it. This hooded robe, white and cotton-textured—passed on from generation to generation—is the traditional attire of Telosian men worn during their coming of age ceremony. It is held close to Andon's frame by a simple twined rope, tied in a single knot about his waist. "Fits perfectly," remarks Neldon, hands partly folded, stroking his beard.

"P'pa," glancing up at Neldon, with his left eye brow raised, "really, you're going to have to stop calling me *that*, you know, especially when Lao is around."

Turning around to face the mirror. "You see that?" pointing to a tuft of hair above his upper lip, maintaining eye contact with the reflection of Neldon in the mirror, "boys don't have those."

"You will always be my dear boy, Andon, but I understand," laughs Neldon. "Yes sir!" snapping into the body posture of a soldier. "Come, it's go time," momentarily staring into blank space, as he mentally calls for a transport pod. "I'll meet you there."

They both walk into the luminescent-white clearing surrounding their dwelling to the sight of a luminescent-white disc-shaped platform about six inches thick and ten feet in diameter, levitating about six inches from the ground, waiting for them.

Andon walks up to the platform and steps unto it. No sooner does he do so than it starts shape-shifting. From the floor of the platform emerges, as if a plant sprouting from its seed deep in the soil, a reclined single-seat sofa with armrests, upon which Andon comfortably relaxes, closing his eyes and giving off a big sigh of relief, "it's show time," saying to himself.

From the perimeter of the platform emerges all around him, a three-inch thick wall which grows outward of the platform's outline to a height of three feet, such that a bowl is formed. It then grows inward to a height of seven feet to form a domed pod, effectively sealing Andon in. The interior of the pod is initially self-lit in white light due to the luminescence of the pod's wall, as well as the floor, all of which are made of the same material, strandanite.

Strandanite is the greatest technological discovery of Telosians, a highly versatile material, made up of programmable carbon based filaments which are orders of magnitude thinner than normal human hair strands. Strandanite is essentially a tubular grouping of microscopic, self-replicating bio-mechanical organisms or nanobots, and feel like the texture of coarse human hair when walked upon. Strandanite multiplies its population through nearly instantaneous reproduction, to create whatever object is required.

Strandanite feeds on the pressure of planetary gravitation, which to it is like standing under a waterfall, mouth wide open. Since its life span is only an infinitesimal fraction of a second, strandanite has to keep reproducing itself to maintain a created form, giving off four inert gasses—alphanon, betanon, gammanon and helium—as waste product. Three of those inert gases become luminous due to planetary gravitation or electric polarisation, which excites them.

Strandanite simply stops reproduction to *uncreate* created objects, when there is no longer need for those objects. Strandanite is grown on a special bed or strandanite carpet, six inches thick. Each bed has a strandanite-based crystal embedded to receive and execute mental instructions. Telosians simply lay strandanite carpets anywhere they choose to dwell, effectively building cities whose streets are miles of luminescent-white strandanite carpet.

The affinity of strandanite for electric polarisation makes it perfect for the instantaneous construction of anti-gravitation pods. The atomic gyroscopic flexibility of strandanite also enables microscopic optical lenses to be formed within walls created by them, fully allowing light in from one direction, mostly reflecting it from the other. Such a convenient invention, used by a very spiritually mature people, has propelled them to the greatest attainment of civilisation.

Andon opens his eyes and makes a gesture with his hand, immediately after which, the wall suddenly becomes perfectly transparent, as if it is not there. All that is left to be seen from inside is the floor of the pod, as well as the seat upon which Andon is comfortably seated.

Neldon waits to observe Andon's departure, as the pod rises rapidly to a height of about five hundred feet in the air, comes to an abrupt stop, and then rapidly shoots off horizontally in a south easterly direction from their home deep in the forests, to Quarters.

Andon's pod arrives over a designated strandanite landing area and comes to an abrupt stop. It then falls out of the sky quite rapidly. At a height of about ten feet above the ground it comes to a sudden stop, and then gently settles on the strandanite ground. The wall loses its transparency and starts to recede, with a gentle white glow, in the exact reverse pattern to how it was erected, till there is nothing left of the pod, leaving Andon sitting out in the open. No sooner does Andon stand up and walk away, than the seat equally fade away in a white glow.

Three boys, identically clothed as Andon, walk over to him to greet him. Jacob, speechless, with his mouth agape and his arms spread out in an inquiring gesture, "What ever was that about, Andon?"

"Er... I was in a... hurry?" replies Andon, scratching his head, rolling his eyes skywards.

"Hoy!" Jacob sighs deeply in resignation, as the rest of them burst into laughter. "Alright fellas," clapping his hands twice, "let's get this over with. Don't know about you, but I've got me a big date tonight. Hey, maybe afterwards, we should—"

"Here they come," interjects Andon, leaning over to catch a better glimpse of four hooded figures—the Telosian high council—equally dressed like the four boys, approaching them on a levitating platform. The fourth individual, Zeekitana, affectionately called Nana Zeeks, is the Telosian planetary logos—a representative of galactic administration to Telos, and oldest living person on the planet.

"Ouma, my dear young men," says Nana Zeeks to the boys, as their levitating platform sets down and dissolves below their feet.

"Ouma, high councillors!" greet the boys in unison.

"Well, aren't you all excited today?" exclaims Nana Zeeks as she breathes in deeply. "It's not at all going to be any different from what you've already rehearsed.

"All you have to do is just smile, wave and bow, really, and I'll do most of the talking.

"Just go through the basic motions and this will be over in no time.

"What's more important, is that you please, remember to... breathe?"

For a moment, there is an awkward silence with everyone looking at each other, wondering what Nana Zeeks is talking about. "I'm talking to you, my dear Andon," so saying as she clutches her chest as if pleading. An outburst of uncontrollable laughter reverberates from the group.

"That's the spirit! Now, gather around and let us be on our way. Everyone is patiently expecting us, let's not keep them waiting any longer," enters Adu, one of the three reps, as she beckons them to form a perfect *circle* of four, centred by the high council. The boys place their hoods over their heads and stand around the leaders, equidistant from each other, and facing in towards them.

On reaching the designated height, the group of eight's open platform repositions overhead a small crowd of family, friends and supporters gathered from all over the planet to witness the ceremony. There is much cheering and applause as the platform arrives overhead. The traditional sound of trumpets joins in with the crowd of people to welcome the initiates, as though a heroes welcome after a long battle.

The feeling of honour and love that Telosian initiates experience on this occasion is one of the incentives that makes it highly desirable to young children, who look forward to it all their lives. It is the recognition of a second birth, one into the ranks of the adults. Since Telosians do not use money, every job required that cannot be done through the use of automation, is done and equally shared by all adult Telosians, according to their chosen careers. They essentially volunteer their skill and time freely, to run their society. The end result is that since there is neither competition nor fear of loss of income, people do not fight to keep a task all to themselves, so as to make them relevant or indispensable.

Telosians only put in sixty hours of official duty per month, and they know not to exceed those hours, even though they would love to. In their free time, they must keep busy in their own way, pursuing whatever interests them. This system has allowed a high degree of culture as well as other desirable qualities to proliferate on Telos. It is also part of the reason why Telosians are eager to travel the universe. They have achieved such a perfected degree of civilisation that it becomes necessary for all to participate in off-world missions to experience mental stimulation, which would otherwise decay should they become too comfortable or complacent in their personal or technical advances.

The roots of the coming of age ceremony on Telos go back to well over eighty thousand years—not long after *the great war* that nearly wiped out Telosians—when space travel to colonise the Telosian moon, Telos Alpha, was at its infancy. Back then they used *explosion propelled* crafts for space travel. Their crafts were designed to harvest hydrogen in real-time from the environment, for use as a propellant.

During that period, Telosians lacked any form of sexual discipline, with all manner of sexual issues which jeopardised the success of extended missions to Telos Alpha, to work at terraforming it. The terraforming personnel, true to Telosian sexual indiscipline, would soon be engaged in endless orgies. There were also constant cases of women being raped, who became too afraid to carry out their tasks.

Where men alone were sent, most of them would soon be sodomising each other, after extended periods away from home. The health problems involved in sodomy rendered them psychologically compromised, and physically useless to carry out the strenuous tasks assigned to them. It was not any better with sending women alone because homosexual activities occurred much easily than in men, albeit with less damage incurred. It was none the less desired that these kinds of activities not happen in the name of Telos. The high council also thought that it was as good a time as any to have sex struck off the list of teething problems which all civilisations experience in their natural onward evolution.

They had already conquered their warring tendencies, the hard way, making the folly of war clear to them all. The end of the great war resulted in the formation of the high council system of leadership, made up of the wisest and most spiritual individuals Telos could offer, to lead and guide them. The formation of the first generation of the Telosian high council triggered the arrival of Nana Zeeks to further help Telosians succeed, since they showed evidence of having grown more mentally mature and genuinely seeking to perfect their human experience, for the greater good of all. Nana Zeeks presence would also guarantee the survival of long-term plans from one high council generation to the next. The role of Nana Zeeks was purely advisory on galactic best-practice. She took no part in decisions or council votes, since that would constitute galactic interference into evolutionary affairs.

The Telosian system of global leadership was extremely transparent, making sure that only those who truly desired the best for Telos would ever be considered for global continental votes to become reps. Reps were forbidden from ever taking a decision, even so much about what time was designated for their meals, without Telosians knowing about it. Reps where the servants of the people and served as a focal point for the collective will of Telosians. They implemented a technologically assisted method of global referendum where all Telosians could vote yes or no in seconds, allowing for very efficient decision making processes by the high council.

The high council came to the conclusion that some necessary steps had to be taken, not just for the sake of the long-term mission to terraform Telos Alpha, but also for the sake of their species' evolution. They then set about to execute a three-step plan that would evolve sexual issues clean out of the Telosian human experience. The high council determined that these three steps would be divided into two phases. The first phase would be *enforced* more strictly with each succeeding generation, and the second phase would be introduced afterwards:

1. Every adult was free to have sexual relations with whomever or whatever pleased their taste, as long as it did not violate criminal codes, such as rape. The only condition was that it must be on public record who is having sexual relations with whom, and that record readily accessible to all. Sexual conduct that was deemed less-than-ideal was *highlighted* on each individual's record. They had the technical means by that time to implement this sexual transparency.

2. A worldwide contraceptive—reproduction vaccine—programme was initiated, mandatory for infants at birth, and adults who wanted it, but by the next generation, the contraceptive programme had caught up with just about every single Telosian. It did not interfere with normal physical development, hormones, or even so much as the menstrual cycles in women. The technique used simply worked to render sperm and ovum themselves useless for reproduction.

Antidotes were administered only after an application was made, and authorisation granted by high council. Used in conjunction with step number one, antidotes were only approved based on the sexual history of individuals. A third infraction through; rape, prostitution, pornographic content creation or even distribution, homosexuality, multiple or simultaneous, rather than single sequential sex partnering, as well as a list of other sexual behaviour which was collectively deemed inimical to their intended sexual evolution, was basis for a life long ban from parenthood, without appeal. In other words, everyone only had room for a maximum of two sexual *slip-ups*. To counterbalance these steps, Nana Zeeks advised the high council that those banned from having children be allowed to adopt orphans, after having demonstrated improvements in their sexual behaviour.

The aim of steps one and two were not punitive, but a long-sighted approach to gently evolving sexual excesses out of Telosians. The premise upon which these steps were based was very simple: Telosians have no business parenting the next generation, if they simply cannot *get a grip* on their sexual activities. People who cannot control themselves may carry on with their ways free of harassment, but those ways *will not* be allowed to live after them.

Generations later, the high council rolled out the second phase of the Telosian sexual evolution plan:

3. Only those who were not banned from parenthood or with a minimum acceptable sexual record, were ever allowed to leave Telos, or set foot upon Telos Alpha. Civilian trips to Telos Alpha by then were getting more frequent, safer, faster and relatively cheap. All Telosians therefore considered a visit to Telos Alpha, at least once in their life time, top of their *bucket list*. This served as an incentive to encourage sexual maturity. Furthermore, a lottery system was introduced to financially assist those who could not afford the cost

of a trip to Telos Alpha. It was, of course, based on sexual records, and only those whose sexual records were *spotless*, were allowed to participate in the lottery.

The recording of sexual infractions by individuals only started counting from the age of accountability that they had in use by then, which was seventeen years of age. It left a window of time in which the seeds of undesired sexual behaviour were sown, prior to the age of accountability, in which all manner of sexual activities were still being engaged in by young adults. It was something which the high council initially thought to overlook, but they realised that once such tastes were developed, it would be difficult to get rid of as adults, making them highly likely to get caught in parental ban.

4. Since punishment through life-long denial of parenthood was not the aim of these steps, but the greater good of the species through adoption of modes of sexual living that represented the highest idea of the collective, it was necessary to create a new accountability system—the fourth and additional step to the original three. They called it the age of sexual accountability, and tagged it at eleven years of age, which coincided with the average age of Telosian children coming into reproductive ability. They still however maintained the original age of accountability in which individuals who committed crimes would be served their idea of justice at the time, to the fullest extent.

In so doing, minors remained minors, the sole responsibility of their parents, but it meant they had to be taught very early in life about the *disadvantages* of participating in certain types of sexual activities among themselves. This was easily achieved with the help of parents, already well self-proved by virtue of their being parents in the first place, and therefore extremely qualified for the task of guiding Telosian children towards ideal sexual behaviour. The children experienced no difficulty in adopting the ideal ways of sexual expression, because they simply emulated their parents who were perfect examples. The high council had essentially made wider, the age range of Telosians accountable for their sexual activities.

The high council further assisted the plan through psychological tactics, used in a beneficial sense. They *glorified* the age of sexual accountability through coming of age ceremonies centred more by boys than girls, with a lot of mouth-watering incentives, such that it made the coming of age ceremonies an extremely desired experience that no Telosian boy was willing to miss out on, for all the temptation in the world. They found it necessary to do so, because they deemed the sodomite proclivities of Telosian men extremely problematic—it died a natural death.

Overall, no shots were fired, no one ever molested, no colour or form of direct force was ever used. It became a situation where all had to simply learn to police themselves. In about a thousand years these steps were redundant, because for Telosians, it was now a way of life, it was their culture, their tradition and they simply knew no other way. The plan simply worked. Sexual desires of individuals were always met in abundance, but in ways that were wholesome, dignified and transparent. Sexual issues simply lost steam, as they worked to rectify other teething evolutionary problems typical of evolving humans on all evolutionary worlds.

There were still some deviations though, but so few and far between. Their overall sexual ideals still remained so supreme that it simply smothered all sexual behaviour that was not in accordance with them, such that deviants soon got tired with themselves, because nobody acknowledged their actions or even wasted a breath in criticism. They simply changed their ways and just partook of what worked.

Telosians of today are technically nudists. To them, the naked body is just that, a naked body. It is not an invitation to sex, it is not considered provocative or even threatening. No one ever swims in public or visits their beaches wearing clothes. *Aquatic affairs* are an entirely *nude affair*, and the Telosians love all things aquatic. Hypocrisy with regard to sex simply does not exist in their consciousness, and the only one who is of sexual interest to them is each their partner. Even on lower level worlds, sex partners simply do not obsess over themselves as long as they regularly satisfy each others sexual needs, which Telosians do, and very, very generously so.

Millennia after millennia, with advancements in

technical knowledge which gave them instantaneous interstellar travel capabilities, all that is left of those extinct steps is that people who *violate* them cannot go to planets at the level of 5.0 or less, were sexual behaviour is still at its evolutionary infancy, and to which they could become tempted to act inappropriately, jeopardising their mission. They did not want a case of leaving behind on lower level worlds, legends of Gods, sons of Gods, or so-called Nephilim, *descending from heaven to sleep with the daughters of men,* in the *holy* name of Telos.

Contraception is now active, rather than the original passive method. When approval is received to conceive a child, couples simply stop eating food items which contain those contraceptives to regain their reproductive abilities. They then resume consumption of them afterwards. Telosians would have it no other way.

Returning to the ceremony. The pod descends into the midst of people gathered, all of whom are seated in a perfect circle, leaving an empty space at the centre for the initiates. On contacting the ground the pod melts into it, and only an outline of the platform remains because it is now revolving at a steady but noticeable speed, making sure that all eight of them standing on it are equally viewed by the entire gathering. The high council lower their hoods, with Nana Zeeks raising her hands in the air, commencing her speech.

"People of Telos," she announces, pressing both

hands against her chest. "It is on occasions such as today's that we're reminded of all that we are.

"What a long, long way we've come from our humble beginning as children born of the jungle, acting like the jungle itself, to a fully matured and enlightened people of cosmic consciousness, fully settled in an endless era of life and light."

"It was not an easy task, ahem, trust me on that one," coughs Nana Zeeks, as the gathering laugh out whole heartedly, understanding her meaning, "but with deliberate effort on each our part, we prevailed," she continues. "Our loving, selfless ways in service to our brethren, children of the universal one, have not gone unnoticed. It has earned us the title of *most beloved* by one and all across the milky way.

"Let us however not rest on our laurels, but persist with thinking those thoughts which bring us ever closer towards the portal of finality, as a galactic custodian and supreme caregiver to our younger brothers and sisters all over the galaxy, on their own journey towards life and light."

The boys are spot-turned a full one hundred and eighty degrees so that each of them now faces the crowd gathered. They lower their hoods and reveal their faces to the gathering, who erupt in cheers.

"Beloved Telosians, my beautiful and wonderful people," continues Nana Zeeks, her voice carrying all over the island, with all listening attentively.

"We are gathered here today, a brand new day for these young men. This day marks the beginning of the rest of their lives as contributing, caregiving citizens of Telos.

"Today, they transition from only being cared for, to giving back care to Telos.

"These young men, of their own free will and as demonstrated by their presence at this ceremony, will pledge *to themselves* before all of you as witnesses, the Telosian oath."

As soon as Nana Zeeks completes her speech, the portion of the revolving platform upon which the boys stand extends upwards to a height of approximately six feet. They then commence the recital of their personal pledge.

"To the universal one, my source of being. Omni-nana-papa, within and without me. Serve all your children through me," they all recite in unison, pressing their right hand against their chest, their left palm pressed against the back of their right hand.

"To the universal one, my source of being. Let me be your instrument of peace," they continue.

"To the universal one, my source of being. Let me be the highest manifestation of thee.

"To the universal one, my source of being. May I be perfect, as you, within and without me, are perfect. So be it."

The boys are lowered back to the ground level of the platform as it revolves. "Which of you young women gathered here today, wishes to share in the pledge with these young men?" Inquires Adu, to the silent gathering.

"I do!"

"I do!" yelps Aisha, Jacob's partner, who jumps out of her seat with her hands flailing about, "I do, I do, I do!" causing restrained laughter within the gathering.

"I do!"

"I do!" Lao lets out, rising up from her seat, pressing her hand against her chest, raising the other. Andon is no longer able to keep a straight face, and smiles from ear to ear.

"Please come forward," beckons Adu to the girls.

The girls emerge from their places in the gathering and walk toward the boys to join them on the revolving platform, as it grows bigger in diameter to accommodate everyone. Andon is reminded of how she makes him feel, as everyday since they fell in love with each other, he has thanked the universe for the good fortune that she is to him.

He breathes in Lao's figure in new light. She is quite the sight to behold all dressed in a white, tight-fitted one-piece suit—the uniform used in space exploration—that leaves only few details of her potently feminine features to his imagination, especially the way she likes to wear that utility belt, sitting all slanted across her waist. He can almost swear that if he did not know any better, Lao's mother, a master geneticist, custom made that body of hers, just for him.

The skin on her face and exposed hands, a light toned chocolate, glowing in the radiation of their sun as she walks towards him, as if in slow motion, reaching over to stow her waist-long hair across her shoulder, threatening to occlude such a perfect view of her modestly sized, gravitation defiant pair of bosoms, mounted on her slender figure and highlighted by her perfectly crafted child-bearing hips. As far as Andon is concerned, she is the most beautiful woman in the whole world, with her oblong face upon which is mounted those soul-piercing pair of eyes, which radiate supreme wisdom and divine intelligence. Her thin lips, a natural reddish-orange, she just licked them... Andon is simply lost for breath, literally!

Lao, the same age as Andon, hails from a long line of prodigious geneticists who have largely spear-headed the genetic upgrade of the Telosian human and animal stocks over long periods—lengthening their average life span—as well as contributed to the perfection of their core technology, strandanite. She too, like most in her family line, will be undergoing apprenticeship to become a geneticist.

"Those are very kind thoughts, Andon," she projects telepathically, shattering his daydream as she takes the last few steps to stand with him, "you honour me." She reaches over with both hands and bends Andon's head towards hers as she kisses his forehead. She then presses her right hand firmly against his chest, as he presses the palm of his right hand against it. She also presses the palm of her left hand against the back of his right hand, as he presses the palm of his left hand against the back of her left hand, all against his chest.

After having shared this type of interlocked and very intimate greeting reserved only for lovers, Lao proceeds to take off his robe, as do the other three girls for their partners. She unties the belt, takes off the robe and places it, neatly folded length-wise, into his held-out arms. She calmly proceeds to remove the emblem from his left upper arm, running her index finger around it in circles till it morphs from what originally looked like it was printed unto his clothing, to a disc-shaped patch, leaving no trace of its removal from the sleeve of his clothing.

Andon starts humming, pointing his nose skywards, rolling his eyes away from Lao in a humorously defiant manner, shattering Lao's solemn atmosphere. He is whistling to the first verse of their favourite song, fire. Lao snorts a burst of restrained laughter as she is caught off guard by Andon's ill-timed antics. She pokes him in the stomach to get him to stop it, only making things worse as Andon jerks forward in laughter, failing to restrain his.

"Ahem!" projects Nana Zeeks telepathically, as she has been observing their activities and is herself not doing very well at restraining her compulsion to join them in laughter, "now, now you two, we're not done yet."

"Our apologies, Nana Zeeks," replies Andon telepathically, on their behalf.

"Those two go back a long way, you know, probably two of the oldest souls on Telos," telepathises Adu to one of her fellow reps, Hibiskia, as they engage themselves in a brief *administrative gossip*.

"Is that so?" replies Hibiskia.

"Indeed. It was Andon who brokered the truce that ended the last great war millennia ago, becoming one of the first reps on Telos. Lao was the geneticist who originally created strandanite. To think they called her all sorts of names. Those two always seem to find themselves across time. There's just no separating them."

Lao retrieves the robe from Andon's hands, placing the patch on one of its sleeves as it immediately dissolves into the fabric, now looking like a printed emblem and leaving no evidence of being attached. She walks over to Nana Zeeks who has erected a table from the revolving platform, upon which Lao places the robe, as do the other girls. Nana Zeeks hands two patches over to Lao, each of which bears an image of a planet being orbited by a space tuber.

Lao presses them to her chest with both hands as she bows down in gratitude to the leaders, who do likewise. She walks up to Andon and hands him one of the patches, she takes the remaining one and places it where she removed the previous one. Andon does likewise attaching the patch to her left upper arm. They once again interlock hands intimately, as they rest their foreheads against each other's. "I go with you," gently whispers Lao. "And I with you, my love," Andon replies. The two emblems signify a voyage into space, and that they will take the journey, together.

"People of Telos!" exclaims Nana Zeeks, "behold, the newest set of care givers. Come, let us welcome and celebrate them together!" so announcing, in a firm tone of finality.

Each of the couples standing side by side, raise and wave their hands and then bow before the gathering, who erupt in a standing ovation. The couples are expressing gratitude to them for coming to witness the ceremony. The platform stops revolving as its outline shrinks in diameter to fit just the leaders, completely detaching from the ground and levitating them away. The couples disperse into the gathering to meet with their families.

"Andon!" a voice rings out, "catch!" but Lao snags it out of the air instead and hands it over to Andon, who walks over to exchange greetings with Lao's parents.

"Oh dear!" exclaims Neldon, "protective instinct or a sharp reflex, Lao?"

"Ouma, Neldon," greets Lao, as she gives him a big hug.

"Ouma, my darling," responds Neldon, hugging Lao as well. "Now, you take care of my little boy for me, will you?" speaking quietly, "you know he is still very sore. Please, always try and talk some sense into that strong-headedness of his." Lao responds with an even tighter hug, fully understanding his meaning.

Looking over to Andon as he returns from Lao's parents', "Your mother had that in storage. She would have wanted you to have it."

"What's on it?" inquires Andon, looking intently at the crystal.

"It contains schematics for a new generation of interplanetary pods with improved... radioactive shiel—

" Neldon pauses for a moment, as he starts to realise that maybe it is not such a bright idea to further fuel Andon's inability to stop grieving his mother. "Amoha planned to complete the design on her return home, and then present it to the high council for approval and mass manufacture.

"It has a technique for additional radioactivity shielding that no one has been able to understand so far. If anyone can figure it out, its going to be you."

"Thank you p'pa," embracing Neldon in gratitude.

"It's okay son, this is all new to me too, and I miss her so terribly," says Neldon, holding Andon in an emotional embrace. "Come here you!" snapping light-heartedly at Lao, as he pulls her into a group hug.

"We're becoming a family now. We have to look ahead and create new memories."

"I love you, Neldon," says Lao. "Thank you for everything."

"It has been my pleasure, dear child," kissing her on her forehead. "Where do you two plan to spend time together, made plans yet?" Neldon inquires of them.

"Telos Alpha, Voltaire falls," replies Lao.

"Excellent choice! Amoha and I spent our first time together over there too. Her recommendation by the way. Who... chose that location, just out of curiosity?" Neldon wonders about the coincidence, since he does not remember mentioning it to Andon.

"Andon did," replies Lao.

"hmm... very interesting indeed. Very, very interesting." losing himself in deep thought. "See, you do think like Amoha. If anyone can solve her puzzle, it'll be you. I guess I know my own son more than he knows himself, eh. We could really use that technique, so *it'll* never happen again."

"I'll do my best, but I give no guarantees," replies Andon, the day's excitement suddenly absent in his tone. "You say I think like her, yet I feel as if... I don't think I'd have taken such a risk if I knew I had loved ones waiting for me," letting out a deep sigh in acceptance. "I guess she saved a planet full of people in the end. That's what really matters, isn't it?" so saying, as he holds the crystal up against the sun, between two fingers, observing its tiny features.

"Maaaybe its time we... you know, be on our way, then?" interjects Lao as she embraces Andon, throwing a glance at Neldon, squinting her eyes at him to drop the topic. It always falls on Lao to put Andon back together, whenever he becomes depressed about his mother's death. Neldon has such a terrible timing.

"Ahh yes, yes, of course! Better to arrive there while the sun is still high," laughing sheepishly, "you two can go for a walk, you know, smell the fresh Alphanian breeze," he remarks hurriedly. He understands Lao's personal challenge with managing Andon's heavy, sometimes selfish emotions. "Safe travels, my children," sharing one last group hug with the couple as he turns around and walks away.

Andon and Lao arrive in a pod at an interplanetary space port. As their pod dissolves around them, they are faced with another pod waiting for them, an interplanetary pod. This particular one is not made of strandanite, but instead of a combination of metals such as gold, lead and mercury which are excellent for anti-gravitation. The result is a dirty-silver, smooth-bodied craft about forty-five feet in diameter, maintaining the signature shape of Telosian pods, but much flatter at its pole.

The pod is fifteen feet tall, and stands upon three small hollow hemispherical domes for its landing gear. The three landing gears double as condensers, each of which generates a harmonic electric field. The three interlocking fields press against each other at their mutual centre underneath the pod, and induce surrounding atmosphere, as if an inverted tornado, with its apex reaching into the pod through an *induction tube* in the centre of the pod.

A flat umbrella-like surface mounted at the top of the pod deflects the inducted vortex radially, through a thin perimeter slot. The result is the familiar *coanda or meissner effect*. The expelled vortex adheres to the skin of the pod, making its way to the bottom of the pod to be re-induced. This multiplies frequencies of induction-expulsion in harmonic multiples with minimal effort, leaving no need for any form of combustion. The preferred dynamics for fast flight by Telosians, is entirely one of implosion, not combustion.

The effect is that gravitation coming from space, is diverted around the pod, leaving it completely weightless, so-called levitation. The glide-away effect of this system also relieves the craft of any form of drag, since air molecules are simply brushed aside and downwards of the pod, never touching it. By stepping up the frequencies of induction relative to expulsion or conduction, interplanetary pods are able to depart a planet's atmosphere in a matter of seconds, and bridge the span of their entire solar system, end to end, in minutes.

A hole appears on the side of the pod and expands into an entrance, which Lao has just mentally opened as they approach the pod. The hole contracts into itself the moment Andon boards the pod behind Lao. Every surface in the cabin is covered in strandanite, and with the exception of the induction pillar which sits right in the middle of the cabin and permanently connected, floor to ceiling, it is a sterile luminescent-white room.

A single-seat sofa, big enough for the two, grows out of the strandanite floor upon which Lao gets comfortable. Out of the floor where Andon stands, a pillar emerges to a height of three and a half feet. The very top surface of the pillar morphs into a hemispherical crystal, upon which Andon places his hand. He breathes in deeply, closing his eyes and bowing his head as if praying. The crystal is the thought-programmable brain of the pod itself.

"Normal, blink of an eye?" mutters Andon to Lao.

"not in a hurry, your call," replies Lao, looking very straight-faced and somewhat unexcited. Their atmosphere has grown thick, she knows Andon very well, and he is not in the mood she would have preferred him to be.

"Bit of both," withdrawing his hand from the control-crystal panel, as it *melts* back into the floor and the interior wall of the pod becomes transparent. "Destination set."

Polarisation of the exterior skin gives off a slightly audible hum as the pod's condensers are charged for departure. The pod shortly comes to a gentle hover about ten feet above the ground. It will be the first time the two have been allowed to leave the planet on their own, as prior to now, they have always had adult supervision. Telosians simply do not leave their children open to risks, by letting them wonder off planet alone.

Andon walks over to the induction pillar and leans against it. "Lao, I have to tell you somethi—"

"It's okay, Andon, I understand. We can always reschedule," Lao cuts in, she has already had her doubts about the trip.

"Is that what you think I wanted to say?" surprised at Lao's response.

"Oh common, Andon, we both know how you get when you dwell on it."

He walks over to her and kneels beside her, grabbing her hands, "I'm the worst, aren't I?" feeling terrible about the situation. "I'm so sorry, Lao, I know how selfish I've been, I know I can be a burden. Yes, nana's gone, but... you're here right now, you're all that matters to me. I just need you to know that. Besides, I more than anyone know how much you've been looking forward to this, and I won't be able to forgive my—"

Lao bursts out laughing, snorting while laughing uncontrollably, tears rolling down her eyes. Her laughter is so infectious, that even Andon joins in. The tense situation immediately loses steam. She reaches over and grabs Andon's arms, pulling him with all her might unto the sofa till Andon lays on top of her and they are face to face, in each other's embrace.

"Aww... that was so sweet, nana's boy," kissing him deeply, "hey, if you remember, I said I would walk with you. Its just you and me," holding Andon's face as she kisses him again, deeply and mercilessly. While locked in each other's embrace, Andon waves his hand, making a gesture.

"No way!" exclaims Lao, "I was wondering why we hadn't lifted off yet!" Andon is playing their favourite music, fire. He suddenly jumps unto his feet, and starts moving energetically, and very seriously to the rhythm. Swinging to the left, swinging to the right, with both hands swinging in opposite directions from that of his torso. Suddenly he jumps in the air, doing a full circle before landing back on his feet.

"Babe, babe, babe, wouldcha light my fire,
wouldcha warm my water,
let me have your fire."

Lao laughs hysterically, clutching her stomach which is now in pain from so much laughter. She did not see this coming, he got her! She claps her hands excitedly like a little girl child, who has just received a birthday present. She jumps unto her feet as well, standing in front of him, mirroring the familiar dance steps as Andon sings along to the karaoke.

Everything about them as far as the eyes can see; from the space port, to the nearby valley, as well as the luminescent-white glow of the strandanite streets and pathways all simply fall away, literally. Their pod has just departed, and has done so rather dramatically. It exits the atmosphere in under ten seconds and then decelerates to a cruise speed. Andon has plans for the ride.

"My babe, babe, wouldcha care to mend my body,

its been cold and lonely,

wouldcha warm my body, babe," Andon continues.

"I was falling and yooou saaaved meee," enters Lao, singing in a voice which sounds like a gentle breeze.

"Babe, babe, babe, babe, babe, babe, babe, babe," replies Andon, flapping his arms like a chicken.

"I'm fiiine when yooou saaave meee," Lao continues.

"Babe, babe, babe, babe, babe, babe, babe, babe," enters Andon again, flapping around ridiculously.

"I looove it when yooou huuug meee."

"Babe, babe, babe, babe, babe, babe, babe,

babe!" lets out Andon, as they dance around in circles all over the cabin.

"Babe babe, babe, wouldcha quench my fire," enters Lao, singing the female portion of the song.

wouldcha chill my water,

you can have my fire.

"Oh babe babe wouldcha care to mend my body,

its been warm and lonely,

wouldcha chill my body, babe."

"I was falling and yoooou saaaved meee," enters Andon, surprisingly, with a well trained voice.

"Babe, babe, babe, babe, babe, babe, babe, babe," replies Lao, dancing around like a chicken and penguin hybrid.

"I'm fiiine when yoooou saaave meee," Andon continues.

"Babe, babe, babe, babe, babe, babe, babe, babe," replies Lao.

"I looove it when yoooou huuug meee," sings Andon.

"Babe, babe, babe, babe, babe, babe, babe,

babe!" Andon and Lao scream out together, proceeding with their antics and personal in-flight entertainment as the pod shoots into the atmosphere of Telos Alpha, not registering even so much as one degree of increase in temperature, for all the speed of its re-entry.

Their pod descends and gently sets down on the edge of a strandanite clearing about two hundred and fifty feet in diameter, nestled close to the edge of Voltaire waterfall, deep in the forests. The crazed couple stumble out of the pod as if intoxicated, laughing profusely. Andon walks a small distance from the pod and places his hand on the control-crystal panel which grows out of the ground as he approaches.

As the pillar with its control-crystal panel dissolves back into the ground, there is a noticeable vibration beneath their feet as a circle outline about a hundred feet in diameter becomes apparent. What follows next is the growth of that circle into a hollow hemisphere as it extends from the ground level, growing narrower in diameter, till it is completely sealed shut at the top, all within the space of a few seconds. This will be the couple's home for the next few days.

As the two approach the structure, an entrance appears to let them in and closes behind them. The interior is fully lit in day light since the wall of the structure is completely transparent from the inside. The interior, as one would expect, is completely bare and awaiting instructions for what to build to make them feel right at home.

Andon takes Lao by her hand, drawing her close to him, raising her chin, both looking into each other's eyes. A gentle kiss he lays upon her soft, sweet lips—wholeness! As if by magic, their clothes dissolve in a white glow. This will not be their first time in such naked proximity, but this one... this one will be different, and always remembered. Andon reaches down, wrapping his arms firmly around Lao's waist as he lifts her up. Her warm body and delicate breasts press against Andon's firm body. Lao instinctively wraps her thighs around Andon's waist, locking them in place with her crossed legs, as if holding on for dear life, with her arms around his neck.

The warmth from Lao's body invigorates Andon, his yearning for her, deepening. The holy moment destined for the two is finally here, and it is worth the pause to savour, as both continue peering into each other's soul. The desire for a deeper sense of oneness with each other grows intense, both hearts pounding louder, but much slower. Andon boards the two-feet thick mattress that emerges at his command, one knee first, then the other, laying his most precious passenger upon it, he, gently upon her, trapped in her unyielding embrace.

They exchange a deep, slow, timeless kiss. The subtle fragrance emanating from behind Lao's ears as Andon kisses her all over, electrifies his brain, and its expanding sensation is unmistakable. Firmly, but gently, Andon thrusts so very deep into Lao's being. "Andon," Lao lets out, lost for breath. The one true love of her soul is firmly within her cradling, nurturing care, he is home. Lao has no desire of ever letting go of this moment, it feels so right to her. How else... with whom else, would she rather have it be.

Andon pauses on his inward thrust, not in a hurry to go anywhere, it is all about this moment of now, nothing else matters. Looking into each other's eyes, the two voicelessly express hope, but in vain, that this shared moment of now will never end. If only ecstasy was not cyclical, he would be content with remaining deep within her, and her around him, *forever*. Andon and his most precious, sweet, kind Lao, finally, one.

Deep into her delicate, innocent being, Andon gently thrusts again, and then again, his technique rhythmic and flawless. This feels so familiar to them, as though this is not their first time together. Gently, respectfully, Andon turns Lao over, her soft buttocks to him, her right leg bent at its knee. Deep into Lao, Andon thrusts again, her eyes rolling deep into their sockets as she nearly faints from delight, clenching her two fists tightly, with Andon's hands within them. "My precious Lao," Andon softly whispers into her ear, as he kisses her all over, one deliberate kiss at a time.

Patiently, gently, firmly, with an experiential maturity beyond their years, Andon and Lao work to render the highest degree of ecstasy to each other. They feel no need to rush, the world can simply wait. As day turns into night, and night turns into day—barely eating, barely drinking, only sleeping and resting in between—the two persist, they simply cannot get enough of each other. Such deepened love, such mutual respect, such dignity. They could ask for nothing more.

After a week has passed and then the next two days go by without the need for any more coupling by the two, only engaging each other in meaningful conversation and making plans for their future together, such as how they would serve, they decide that it is perhaps time to rejoin society and proceed, together, with the next phase of their lives as apprentices to their respective fields of interest.

On arrival back at Telos, Andon and Lao still live

apart with their respective families, occasionally getting together to be alone with each other. They dedicate time to their studies, as well as assist the elders of Telos with the tutelage of children. Telosians particularly desire this sort of interaction of new young couples with children, because it elicits a healthy sense of envy in them, making the children desirous of being like them—celebrated and liberated—even while still being under the care of their parents, and still answerable to them for some time yet.

The success of Telos as a civilisation, in general, is based upon transparency. If there is something one desires to do which they cannot or must not let others know about, then it means that something ill advised is being undertaken. They understand this very much, as well as the fact that all needs must be met. This understanding has enabled them create an environment where no one has to do anything in secret. It breeds correctness and innocence of mind, consistent with their self-chosen ideals.

To the uninitiated onlooker, Telosians appear to be a sexually stoic human species, but that is not due to a lack of interest in sex, it is due completely to being sexually satisfied. While they are not without other evolutionary challenges—many of which have been solved enough to give them the high ranking of a 9.2 level planet—sex in general is simply *not* one of them, for they conquered it tens of thousands of years ago, through a deliberate and enlightened approach.

Bonus

Andon and Lao are now twenty two years old. They have long completed their apprenticeship and very competent in their respective fields. Andon has his desire to be stationed in earth's system granted. They arrive earth in a cloaked space tuber and take an orbit around earth's moon.

They work round the clock in their service to earth, doing everything from neutralising radioactivity from nuclear power stations, accumulating in its upper atmosphere, to monitoring the general health of those same power stations with permanently stationed autonomous telemetry pods, which alerts them to the possibility of a radioactive thermal runaway.

On many occasions, they have had to go in and intervene, well before the nuclear power stations' operators even suspect that something is wrong. They then send anonymous messages to the engineers concerned, alerting them to flaws which immediately need to be fixed. Andon and Lao have never understood the logic behind placing nuclear power plants close to fault lines, or by the coast. They can only assume that either it is deliberate mischief, or perhaps those who planned the construction of these power stations simply did not know any better.

In one incident where an earthquake resulted in a tsunami that decimated an entire city, they went in and simply made the nuclear fuel materials disappear, well before the station got hit by the tsunami. They assisted with relocating as many people as possible out of harm's way and dropping them off elsewhere, clear of the tsunami, without letting them know that they were just assisted. Lao and her team of geneticist work hard at repairing genetic defects in flora and fauna, especially those in the vicinity of nuclear power stations.

They have also supplied intelligence to relevant persons, who can do something about it, to prevent the deliberate setting off of nuclear wars, which is survivable by none, not even in the underground bunkers. They have occasionally received exceptions to the non-interference rule and overtly terminated attempts to use nuclear devices. They routinely frustrate attempts to weaponise space, even as they babysit astronauts in orbit, secretly intervening where necessary to ensure their survival while in friendly space.

Over the past year since Andon and Lao's arrival in earth's system, Andon has grown interested in a young lady, and observes her activities when ever he completes his patrol duties in his pod, before returning to the mother ship. He is prone to being sloppy about the invisibility of his pod. More than once, his pod has been photographed, when it should have been invisible. The pods interest in a particular *rough area* has been the subject of debate in the news media.

It so happens that Andon is curious about a sixteen year old high school drop out. She is a cocaine addict and HIV positive, with a fetish for being gang-raped. The young woman, Christine, has managed to scrape up enough money to pay for her *fix* near an abandoned factory. She is being watched by two men who wait for her to be fully intoxicated, so that they can rape her. They have heard her story and know she will not resist them.

"Andon!" grabbing him from behind. Lao hopes she can talk him out of doing something stupid. "...and what are you going to do when you get there?" she inquires.

"I'll do what I have to, Lao," turning around to embrace her. "She's at her limit, if nothing is done, she's going to die, again."

"It's still interference, Andon, more so a very personal one," says Lao, "also, your judgement... you're not yourself right now and you know it!"

Andon realises this truth. He tears himself from her, pacing about, looking for a loop hole in her logic. "Well, was it interference when she saved them?" looking at Lao coldly, visibly upset. "How many more times does she have to die from abandonment? Would you abandon me too, if I got myself into trouble, huh, Lao? Would you?"

"Don't be like this Andon!" clutching her chest, shocked at his question "please, I... I just have a bad feeling about this." Lao has never seen Andon like this before, she is simply unprepared for this. Andon's mind is made up, and he is going to save Christine. Lao knows that she is powerless to change his mind, especially with

Christine being involved.

He takes one step into the pod, barely able to look back at Lao as she cries. "Please, just let me have this one, I beg of you. I'll fix her, and then we can go home. We'll leave this system and never return, I will go with you, Lao." Andon boards the pod and the entrance is sealed behind him. He departs the hangar of their mother ship, locking in on the telemetry pod that he sent to monitor Christine. He arrives there momentarily.

Christine is already being gang-raped, and this time she is unconscious from an overdose. He disembarks the pod mid-air using his utility belt, which also functions as an anti-gravitation device. He enters the scene, silently descending behind the men. "Trenton!" he calls out, "that'll be enough!"

The two men are extremely frightened by his sudden appearance seemingly out of nowhere, one so much so, that he immediately takes flight. There is no way that Trenton is going to run away now, since his name is known to Andon, whom he presumes to be a fellow earth person. He withdraws from Christine, calmly zips up, and then buckles his belt.

He pulls out his cell phone, pointing its flash light at Andon's face. "'Sup pretty boy! You lost or somin'?" so saying, as he walks calmly towards Andon while reaching for his concealed knife. He also looks Andon over carefully, for signs of a concealed weapon. "Nice tights. What are you... like, Clark Kent?"

"Oh, that's just original, Trenton, very nice," replies Andon, reaching over to the sleeve of his right upper arm, pinching it to extract a capsule. "This is your last warning, just... go home. We can forget this ever happened, but I need to attend to Christine, right now." Making his way to Christine by walking around, and well clear of Trenton, "What you're thinking right now... terrible idea."

"Oh I see. So you're like... you're like a hero, right, savin' the damsel in distress 'n all them shit you mother fucking faggot!" Trenton is having none of this, he will not be ignored, and charges at Andon, who now has his back exposed to him, but simply falls to the ground in a full-bodied spasmodic fit.

"Better sleep this one out," remarks Andon, who does not even bother looking back at Trenton as he stands over Christine's unconscious, naked body. There is no way Trenton could have known that Andon's invisible anti-gravitation field was still active, and set-to-stun. He is immediately electrocuted and rendered unconscious, as his metallic knife contacts the field.

Andon reaches over to his utility belt and deactivates the field surrounding him, so that he can handle Christine. He gets down on one knee beside her, prying her mouth open to place the capsule inside, gently forcing her to crush it with her teeth, at least once. He carries her and sets her down against a pile of discarded vehicle tyres.

Andon reaches over to his right upper arm, and grows a thin frequency generator stylus out of the fabric of his suit. He picks up Christine's blouse which was ripped off from her body, sits down beside her and starts to mend it, reattaching the ripped portions at the molecular level. Christine gradually awakens, watching him. "Who are you?" barely able to speak.

Andon sighs, not even able to look at her, "family," shaking his head, holding back tears. "I'm your family, Christine."

"Grew up in an orphanage, don't have… family" she mutters very weakly, "what did you do to me?"

"Just a detox," Andon replies gently, "it'll clean you up and you'll be as good as new in a few hours. Listen, Christine, I'm leaving. I won't be here to help you, you've just got to put yourself back together," he continues, as he mends her blouse. "You're so much greater than you know—Here, put this on," helping her with her blouse. "Its getting chilly out here."

"Do I know you… from… somewhere?" Christine inquires inaudibly, not sure what to make of Andon's kindness.

Andon laughs, crying at the same time, shaking his head. "Let's get your pants back on, I'm going to take you home." He slips on her trousers as far as they can go while she sits there on the cold ground, and just as he is about to help her on her feet to get her fully dressed, a series of cracks can be heard in the distance. Three red spots appear on Andon's suit, growing bigger. It was a trap, they got him!

Andon falls to his knees, clutching his bullet-ridden chest with both hands, his palms soaked in his own blood, the look of horror and intense pain all over his face. Andon simply cannot believe what has just happened. He looks at Christine who is rocking compulsively, back and forth, moaning as she does, too weak to scream, his blood on her face. "It's not... your fault," choking on his own blood, "it's not your—" Bang! Andon's head jerks sideways, very violently, this time the sniper being much closer. He is dead before he hits the ground.

To be continued?

Contact Information:

Email: Sidl234@yahoo.com